Workshop on Computational Linguistics for Literature

(CLfL 2013)

Atlanta, Georgia, USA
14 June 2013

ISBN: 978-1-62993-008-4

Printed from e-media with permission by:

Curran Associates, Inc.
57 Morehouse Lane
Red Hook, NY 12571

Some format issues inherent in the e-media version may also appear in this print version.

Printed by Curran Associates, Inc. (2013)

Association for Computational Linguistics
209 N. Eighth Street
Stroudsburg, Pennsylvania 18360

Phone: 1-570-476-8006
Fax: 1-570-476-0860

acl@aclweb.org

Additional copies of this publication are available from:

Curran Associates, Inc.
57 Morehouse Lane
Red Hook, NY 12571 USA
Phone: 845-758-0400
Fax: 845-758-2634
Email: curran@proceedings.com
Web: www.proceedings.com

A word from the organizers

Welcome to the second edition of our young but vibrant workshop on Computational Linguistics for Literature. We are thrilled to have been able to accept a pleasantly wide range of interesting papers on the computational treatment of literature. The ACL community is certainly embracing literature!

We want the workshop to bring together NLP researchers interested in literature and literary scholars on the quantitative edge of their field. We feel that those who "count words" for a living have something to offer to people who "read books" for a living, and *vice versa*. As Rauscher *et al.* (this volume) put it:

> It is hard for the computer scientist to imagine what research questions form the discourse in the humanities. In contrast to this, humanities scholars have a hard time imagining the possibilities and limitations of computer technology...

Most papers at this year's workshop touch upon the mutual benefits of interdisciplinary examination and the hurdles between computational methods and literary analysis. Two papers discuss such issues directly. Hammon *et al.* share their experience of combining literary analysis and computation in an annotation project. They emphasize the advantages of such collaboration. Boot discusses the importance of research into how literary works are perceived by their audiences and how a corpus of written "responses" can be a useful and interesting resource. This line of research, if further developed, may help gain insights into the role of the reader in the literary process – and help show the way toward modeling that role computationally.

Two papers look at similar problems: how NLP can be effective in exploring and comparing differences between genres, and in testing certain literary hypotheses. Rauscher *et al.* show that extended analysis of concordances helps gain literary insight; and Jautze *et al.* use syntax as the basis of informative stylometric analysis across genres.

Like last year, the computational treatment of poetry takes the central role at the workshop: five of ten papers! Voigt and Jurafsky perform a diachronic study of how the 20th-century political history of China has affected the country's poetic tradition. Asgari and Chappelier apply topic modeling to a corpus of Persian poems and demonstrate that their methodology can contribute to comparative literature studies. Almuhareb *et al.* work on distinguishing Arabic poems from prose, and develop a search engine for Arabic poetry. The other two papers deal with high-level topical analyses of poetry, and point out significant challenges in this task. Fournier describes a pilot study into topical segmentation of Coleridge's Kubla Khan; Brooke *et al.* build upon their previous work on topical segmentation of T. S. Eliot's The Waste Land in an attempt to automatically cluster its segments by their speakers.

At the symbolic end of the spectrum this year, Lessard and Levison explore the process of constructing a graphical representation of a story's event structure to examine the role of repetition. They find the directed acyclic graph (DAG) to be a formalism that captures the intersecting threads of time and action in the film *Groundhog Day*.

Finally, we are honored to host two distinguished speakers for a pair of invited talks. Livia Polanyi, Consulting Professor of Linguistics at Stanford University, has made longstanding contributions to the study of narrative, computational linguistics, discourse theory and related fields. Mark Riedl, Assistant Professor in the Georgia Tech School of Interactive Computing and director of its Entertainment Intelligence Lab, is an expert in the emerging field of interactive narrative and its relationship with the study of textual narrative.

It is already the second edition of our workshop, and yet we are still only just scratching the surface of what interesting computational and humanistic problems – and solutions – are found in the collaboration of computational linguistics and literary analysis... Enjoy!

Anna, David and Stan

Program Committee

Apoorv Agarwal, Columbia University
Cecilia Ovesdotter Alm, Rochester Institute of Technology
Nate Chambers, United States Naval Academy
Nicholas Dames, Columbia University
Anna Feldman, Montclair State University
Mark Finlayson, MIT
Pablo Gervás, Universidad Complutense de Madrid
Amit Goyal, University of Maryland
Catherine Havasi, MIT Media Lab
Jerry Hobbs, University of Southern California
Justine Kao, Stanford University
Kathy McKeown, Columbia University
Inderjeet Mani, Yahoo Labs!
Rada Mihalcea, University of North Texas
Saif Mohammad, National Research Council, Canada
Vivi Nastase, FBK Trento
Rebecca Passonneau, Columbia University
Livia Polanyi, Stanford University
Michaela Regneri, Saarland University
Reid Swanson, University of California, Santa Cruz
Marilyn Walker, University of California, Santa Cruz
Janyce Wiebe, University of Pittsburgh
Bei Yu, Syracuse University

Invited Speakers

Livia Polanyi, Stanford University
Mark Riedl, Georgia Tech

Organizers

David Elson, Google
Anna Kazantseva, University of Ottawa
Stan Szpakowicz, University of Ottawa

The papers

The schedule

9:00	Welcome
9:00-10:00	Invited talk 1 *Reflections on Verbal Art 40 years after* Livia Polanyi
10:00-10:30	*A Tale of Two Cultures: Bringing Literary Analysis and Computational Linguistics Together* Adam Hammond, Julian Brooke and Graeme Hirst
10:30-11:00	Coffee break
11:00-11:30	*Recognition of Classical Arabic Poems* Abdulrahman Almuhareb, Ibrahim Alkharashi, Lama Al Saud and Haya Altuwaijri
11:30-12:00	*Tradition and Modernity in 20th Century Chinese Poetry* Rob Voigt and Dan Jurafsky
12:00-12:30	*Linguistic Resources and Topic Models for the Analysis of Persian Poems* Ehsaneddin Asgari and Jean-Cedric Chappelier
12:30-14:00	Lunch break
14:00-15:00	Invited talk 2 *Intelligent Narrative Generation: From Cognition to Crowdsourcing* Mark Riedl
15:00-15:30	Poster teasers *The desirability of a corpus of online book responses* Peter Boot *Clustering Voices in The Waste Land* Julian Brooke, Graeme Hirst and Adam Hammond *An initial study of topical poetry segmentation* Chris Fournier *Groundhog DAG: Representing Semantic Repetition in Literary Narratives* Greg Lessard and Michael Levison *Exploring Cities in Crime: Significant Concordance and Co-occurrence in Quantitative Literary Analysis* Janneke Rauscher, Leonard Swiezinski, Martin Riedl and Chris Biemann
15:30-16:00	Coffee break
16:00-16:30	Poster session
16:30-17:00	*From high heels to weed attics: a syntactic investigation of chick lit and literature* Kim Jautze, Corina Koolen, Andreas van Cranenburgh and Hayco de Jong
17:00-17:30	An informal presentation *Identification of Speakers in Novels* Hua He, Denilson Barbosa and Greg Kondrak
17:30	Farewell

Invited speaker 1

Livia Polanyi joined Stanford University in 2012 as Consulting Professor of Linguistics after leaving Microsoft Corporation where she was a Principal Researcher at Bing working on applications of formal theories of discourse structure to problems in search. She also taught at the University of Amsterdam, Rice University and the University of Tel Aviv, and held scientist positions in computational linguistics at BBN Labs, Fuji-Xerox Palo Alto Labs and Powerset Corporation where she was the first member of the technical team. Professor Polanyi's research focusses on the structure of language above the sentence and she has published work in theoretical, socio and computational linguistics as well as in literary theory, anthropology, economics and political science. Currently she is working on extensions of formal concepts developed to account for discourse interpretability despite discontinuity to foundational problems in music, dance and conversation. She is also a poet.

Reflections on Verbal Art 40 years after

Abstract

Many years ago, a young girl who dared not call herself a "poet" sat alone at her desk day after day writing texts that she dared not call "poems". Each text, she knew, was a little theory about the nature of language. Once the text began, she simply did what was required. The artist is servant not mistress, she had learned. Creation is strictly carrying out what one is told. It was a lonely life. No one saw the words that she wrote. As a foot soldier in the army of those who wrote for the desk drawer, she talked to herself and grew impatient with what she had to say and so she decided one day to leave her desk and go out into the world beyond the window, to read instead of write and to listen to what others had to say. She wanted to understand what she had been doing day after day at her desk near the window because she knew that what had been happening there was that literature was being born – not great literature, probably not even good literature – and she wanted to know what this "literature" she was so busy serving might be. And so, she began to study the nature of language and to put off all consideration of what on earth that girl behind the window had been doing. She read and she studied and she learned and eventually she wrote and she explained and she taught and she left behind the questions about the nature of literature that had sent her out in the world to understand.

But the years have a way of catching up with everyone and as summers became winters and winters became summers again, the young girl became a young woman and then a woman no longer young and then again that young woman no longer young found herself alone at a desk writing texts the she dared not call "poems" but now as she wrote as the theories flowed out onto the page she had learned enough to understand what these texts were theories of and why and how the language of the first breath that would grow into a full text determined the possibilities of what that text could become. And so, in this talk, having been asked to talk to this workshop on computational approaches to literature I will share with you some speculations about the nature of Verbal Art that I have learned through study and practice in the years that separated the woman who will stand before you from that young girl who sat behind her desk near a window years and years ago and wrote down texts that she did not give the name that they had earned.

Invited speaker 2

Mark Riedl is an Assistant Professor in the Georgia Tech School of Interactive Computing and director of the Entertainment Intelligence Lab. Dr. Riedl's research focuses on the intersection of artificial intelligence, virtual worlds, and storytelling. The principle research question Dr. Riedl addresses through his research is: how can intelligent computational systems reason about and autonomously create engaging experiences for users of virtual worlds and computer games. Dr. Riedl earned a PhD degree in 2004 from North Carolina State University, where he developed intelligent systems for generating stories and managing interactive user experiences in computer games. From 2004 to 2007, Dr. Riedl was a Research Scientist at the University of Southern California Institute for Creative Technologies where he researched and developed interactive, narrative-based training systems. Dr. Riedl joined the Georgia Tech College of Computing in 2007 and in 2011 he received a DARPA Young Faculty Award for his work on artificial intelligence, narrative, and virtual worlds. His research is supported by the NSF, DARPA, the U.S. Army, and Disney.

Intelligent Narrative Generation: From Cognition to Crowdsourcing

Abstract

Storytelling is a pervasive part of the human experience–we as humans tell stories to communicate, inform, entertain, and educate. But what about computational systems? There are many applications for which we would also like intelligent system to reason about, understand, and create narrative structures: from recognition to question-answering, from entertainment to education. In this talk I will look at one particular aspect of computational modeling of narrative: automated story generation, the problem of creating novel narrative fabula event sequences for dramatic, pedagogical, or other purposes. I will trace the evolution of fabula story generation from its roots in cognitive systems to data-driven techniques and crowdsourcing. I will speculate on how systems may eventually learn how to create and tell stories from interacting with humans and literature.

A Tale of Two Cultures: Bringing Literary Analysis and Computational Linguistics Together

Adam Hammond
Dept of English
University of Toronto
adam.hammond@utoronto.ca

Julian Brooke
Dept of Computer Science
University of Toronto
jbrooke@cs.toronto.edu

Graeme Hirst
Dept of Computer Science
University of Toronto
gh@cs.toronto.edu

Abstract

There are cultural barriers to collaborative effort between literary scholars and computational linguists. In this work, we discuss some of these problems in the context of our ongoing research project, an exploration of free indirect discourse in Virginia Woolf's *To The Lighthouse*, ultimately arguing that the advantages of taking each field out of its "comfort zone" justifies the inherent difficulties.

1 Introduction

Within the field of English literature, there is a growing interest in applying computational techniques, as evidenced by the growth of the Digital Humanities (Siemens et al., 2004). At the same time, a subfield in Computational Linguistics that addresses a range of problems in the genre of literature is gaining momentum (Mani, 2013). Nevertheless, there are significant barriers to true collaborative work between literary and computational researchers. In this paper, we discuss this divide, starting from the classic rift between the two cultures of the humanities and the sciences (Snow, 1959) and then focusing in on a single aspect, the attitude of the two fields towards ambiguity. Next, we introduce our ongoing collaborative project which is an effort to bridge this gap; in particular, our annotation of Virginia Woolf's *To the Lighthouse* for free indirect discourse, i.e. mixtures of objective narration and subjective speech, requires a careful eye to literary detail, and, while novel, interacts in interesting ways with established areas of Computational Linguistics.

2 Background

2.1 The "Two Cultures" Problem

Since the publication of C. P. Snow's influential *The Two Cultures and the Scientific Revolution* (Snow, 1959), the phrase "the two cultures" been used to signify the rift—perceived and generally lamented—between scientific and humanities intellectual cultures. The problem, of course, is the ignorance of each culture with regard to the methods and assumptions of the other, and the resulting impossibility of genuine dialogue between them, preventing them from working together to solve important problems. Many scholars describing the recent rise of the Digital Humanities—the area of research and teaching concerned with the intersection of computing and humanities disciplines—have argued that it effects a reconciliation of the two alienated spheres, bringing scientific methodology to bear on problems within the humanities, many of which had previously been addressed in a less-than-rigorous manner (Hockey, 2004).

From within the discipline of English literature, however, the application of computational methods to literary analysis has frequently been—and continues to be—a matter of considerable controversy (Hoover, 2007; Flanders, 2009). This controversy arises from the perception of many traditional humanists that computational analysis, which aims to resolve dilemmas, seeking singular truth and hard-and-fast answers, is incompatible with the aims of humanistic research, which is often focused on opening up questions for debate rather than resolving them decisively, and often premised on the idea that there are no right answers, only well- and poorly-supported arguments. Critics have responded to these views by arguing that the best computational literary analysis participates in this project of opening up meaning, arguing that it is not a rejection of literary reading but rather a method for carrying it out more efficiently and extending it to more texts (Ramsay, 2007), and that computational modelling, even when unsuccessful, allows for the application of the scientific method and thus carries the potential for intellectual advancement not possible with purely anecdotal evidence (McCarty, 2005). Despite such counter-arguments, however, the fear remains widespread among traditional literary scholars that the rise of computational analysis will entail the loss of certain sacred assumptions of humanistic inquiry.

2.2 Ambiguity Across the "Cultures"

We argue, though, that these fears are not without basis, particularly when one considers the very different approaches to the question of ambiguity in the two specific disciplines involved in our project: English Literature and Computational Linguistics. Here, the rift of the two cultures remains evident.

A major focus of literary scholarship since the early twentieth century has been the semantic multiplicity of literary language. Such scholarship has argued that literature, distinct from other forms of discourse, may be deliberately ambiguous or polysemous and that literary analysis, distinct from other analytic schools, should thus aim not to resolve ambiguity but to describe and explore it. This was a central insight of the early twentieth-century school, the New Criticism, advanced in such works as William Empson's *Seven Types of Ambiguity* (Empson, 1930) and Cleanth Brooks's *The Well Wrought Urn* (Brooks, 1947), which presented ambiguity and paradox not as faults of style but as important poetic devices. New Criticism laid out a method of literary analysis centred on the explication of the complex tensions created by ambiguity and paradox, without any effort to resolve them. Also in the first half of the twentieth century, but independently, the Russian critic Mikhail Bakhtin developed his theory of dialogism, which valorized "double-voiced" or polyphonic works that introduce multiple, competing perspectives—particularly voices—that present conflicting ideologies (Bakhtin, 1981). Bakhtin, who wrote his seminal work "Discourse in the Novel" under a Stalinist sentence of exile, particularly valued works that enacted the free competition of ideologically opposed voices. In a similar spirit, but independently of Bakhtin, the German critic Erich Auerbach described the "multi-personal representation of consciousness", a narrative technique in which the writer, typically the narrator of objective facts, is pushed entirely into the background and the story proceeds by reflecting the individual consciousnesses of the characters; Auerbach argued that this was a defining quality of modernist (early twentieth-century) literature (Auerbach, 1953). In the second half of the twentieth century, this critical emphasis on ambiguity and paradox developed in an extreme form into the school of deconstructive criticism, which held a theory of the linguistic sign according to which determinate linguistic meaning is considered logically impossible. Deconstructive literary analysis proceeds by seeking out internal contradictions in literary texts to support its theory of infinitely ambiguous signification.

In Computational Linguistics, by contrast, ambiguity is almost uniformly treated as a problem to be solved; the focus is on disambiguation, with the assumption that one true, correct interpretation exists. In the sphere of annotation, for instance, there is an expectation that agreement between annotators, as measured by statistics such as kappa (Di Eugenio and Glass, 2004), reach levels (generally 0.67 or higher) where disagreements can be reasonably dismissed as noise; the implicit assumption here is that subjectivity is something to be minimized. The challenge of dealing with subjectivity in CL has been noted (Alm, 2011), and indeed there are rare examples in the field where multiple interpretations have been considered during evaluations—for instance, work in lexical cohesion (Morris and Hirst, 2005) and in using annotator disagreements as an indicator that two words are of similar orientation (Taboada et al., 2011)—but they are the exception. Work in CL focused on literary texts tends towards aspects of the texts which readers would not find particularly ambiguous, for example identifying major narrative threads (Wallace, 2012) or distinguishing author gender (Luyckx et al., 2006).

3 A Collaborative Research Agenda

The obvious solution to the problem of the "two cultures"—and one that has often been proposed (Friedlander, 2009)—is interdisciplinary collaboration. But while there are many computational linguists working in literary topics such as genre, and many literary scholars performing computational analysis of literature, genuine collaboration between the disciplines remains quite rare. Over the past two years, we have undertaken two collaborative projects—one mostly complete, one ongoing—which aim at such genuine collaboration, and in so doing seek to bridge the real rift between scientific and humanities cultures.[1] Each of these projects is multi-faceted, seeking (a) to produce meaningful research within both disciplines of Computational Linguistics and English Literature; (b) to provide educational experience which broadens the disciplinary horizons of the undergraduate students involved in the projects; and (c) to provide a model of collaborative research that will spur further such "culture-spanning" projects.

Each of our projects was launched in the context of a course entitled "The Digital Text" offered by the Department of English at the University of Toronto. The first author, whose background is in English Literature, is instructor of the course, while the second author, a graduate student in Computer Science, was assigned as a teaching assistant. Working together with the third author, we have designed these projects collaboratively.

The first project, which we call "He Do the Police in Different Voices",[2] was carried out in 2011–12 (Hammond, 2013). Focused on a "multipersonal" poem, *The Waste Land* (1922) by T.S. Eliot, it encompassed each of the three aspects of our projects outlined above; in particular, it was motivated by a research question of interest to both disciplines: could we identify the points in *The Waste Land* where the style changes, where one "voice" gives way to another? A computational approach promised to bring added rigor as well as a degree of objectivity to this question, which humanities methods had proven unable to resolve in almost a century of debate. Both because poetry is dense in signification, and because the multiple voices in *The Waste Land* are a deliberate effect achieved by a single author rather than a disguised piecing together of the works of multiple authors, the question provided a meaningful challenge to the computational approach, an unsupervised vector-space model which first segments by identifying points of stylistic change (Brooke et al., 2012) and then clusters the resulting segments together into voices (Brooke et al., 2013).

This research project was tightly integrated into the curriculum of "The Digital Text". Students were instructed in the use of the Text Encoding Initiative (TEI) XML guidelines,[3] and each of the students provided one annotation related to voice as part of a marked assignment. Students also participated in an online poll in which they indicated every instance in which they perceived a vocal switch in the poem, and their responses were used in the construction of a gold standard for the evaluation of our computational approach.

Once they were complete, we developed our results into a publicly accessible website.[4] This website promises to encourage collaboration between literary scholars and computational linguists by explaining the project and our results in language accessible to both, and by producing a new digital edition of the poem based on our findings. Human and computer readings of the poem are presented side-by-side on the website, to demonstrate that each interprets the poem in different ways, but that neither of these methods is absolutely valid. Rather, we encourage website visitors to decide for themselves where they believe that the vocal switches occur, and we provide an interactive interface for dividing the poem up according to their own interpretation. In addition to serving as a model of collaboration between English Literature and Computational Linguistics—and also serving as a teaching tool for instructors of *The Waste Land* at any level—the site is thus useful to us as a source of further data.

[1] In addition, the third author was part of a separate collaborative project between our departments (Le et al., 2011), though the aim of that project was not literary analysis.

[2] This is a reference to Eliot's working title for *The Waste Land*, which in itself is a reference to a talented storyteller in *Our Mutual Friend* by Charles Dickens; another Dickens novel is alluded to in the title of this paper.

[3] http://www.tei-c.org/Guidelines/

[4] http://www.hedothepolice.org

4 The "Brown Stocking" Project

4.1 Free Indirect Discourse in *To the Lighthouse*

Our second, ongoing project, "The Brown Stocking", focuses on a literary text deliberately chosen for its deeply ambiguous, polysemous, dialogic nature: Virginia Woolf's (1927) *To the Lighthouse* (*TTL*). Woolf's novel was produced at the same time that critical theories of ambiguity and polyvocality were being developed, and indeed was taken as a central example by many critics. Our project takes its title from the final chapter of Erich Auerbach's *Mimesis*, in which Auerbach presents *TTL* as the representative text of modernist literature's "multipersonal representation of consciousness" (Auerbach, 1953). For Auerbach, there are two principal distinguishing features in Woolf's narrative style. The first is the tendency, already noted, to "reflect" incidents through the subjective perspectives of characters rather than presenting them from the objective viewpoint of the author; thus *TTL* becomes a work in which there is more than one order and interpretation. Woolf's technique not only introduces multiple interpretations, however, but also blurs the transitions between individual perspectives, making it difficult to know in many instances who is speaking or thinking.

Woolf achieves this double effect—multiple subjective impressions combined with obscuring of the lines separating them from the narrator and from one another—chiefly through the narrative technique of free indirect discourse (also known as free indirect style). Whereas direct discourse reports the actual words or thoughts of a character, and indirect discourse summarizes the thoughts or words of a character in the words of the entity reporting them, free indirect discourse (FID) is a mixture of narrative and direct discourse (Abrams, 1999). As in indirect discourse, the narrator employs third-person pronouns, but unlike indirect discourse, the narrator includes words and expressions that indicate subjective or personalized aspects clearly distinct from the narrator's style. For example, in the opening sentences of *TTL*:

> "Yes, of course, if it's fine tomorrow," said Mrs. Ramsay. "But you'll have to be up with the lark," she added. To her son these words conveyed an extraordinary joy, as if it were settled, the expedition were bound to take place, and the wonder to which he had looked forward, for years and years it seemed, was, after a night's darkness and a day's sail, within touch.

we are presented with two spans of objective narration (*said Mrs. Ramsay* and *she added*) and two passages of direct discourse, in which the narrator introduces the actual words of Mrs. Ramsay (*"Yes, of course, if it's fine tomorrow"* and *"But you'll have to be up with the lark"*). The rest of the passage is presented in FID, mixing together the voices of the narrator, Mrs. Ramsay, and her son James: while the use of third-person pronouns and the past tense and clearly indicates the voice of the narrator, phrases such as *for years and years it seemed* clearly present a subjective perspective.

In FID's mixing of voices, an element of uncertainty is inevitably present. While we can be confident of the identity of the voice speaking certain words, it remains unclear whether other words belong to the narrator or a character; in this case, it is not clear whether *for years and years it seemed* presents James's actual thoughts, Mrs. Ramsay's summary of her son's thoughts, the narrator's summary of James's thoughts, the narrator's summary of Mrs. Ramsay's summary of James's thoughts, etc. Abrams (1999) emphasizes uncertainty as a defining trait of FID: the term "refers to the way, in many narratives, that the reports of what a character says and thinks shift in pronouns, adverbs, and grammatical mode, as we move—or sometimes hover—between the direct narrated reproductions of these events as they occur to the character and the indirect representation of such events by the narrator". FID, with its uncertain "hovering", is used throughout *TTL*; it is the principal technical means by which Woolf produces ambiguity, dialogism, and polysemy in the text. It is thus the central focus of our project.

In Literary Studies, Toolan (2008) was perhaps the first to discuss the possibility of automatic recognition of FID, but his work was limited to a very small, very informal experiment using a few *a priori* features, with no implementation or quantitative analysis of the results. Though we are not aware of work in Computational Linguistics that deals with this kind of subjectivity in literature—FID is included in the narrative annotation schema of Mani (2013), but it is not given any particular attention within that framework—there are obvious connections with sentence-level subjectivity analysis (Wilson et al., 2005) and various other stylistic tasks, including authorship profiling (Argamon et al., 2007). Since the subjective nature of these passages is often expressed through specific lexical choice, it would be interesting to see if sentiment dictionaries (Taboada et al., 2011) or other stylistic lexical resources such as dictionaries of lexical formality (Brooke et al., 2010) could be useful.

4.2 Our Approach

Our project is proceeding in four stages: an initial round of student annotation, a second round of student annotation, computational analysis of these annotations, and the development of a project website. In the first stage, we had 160 students mark up a passage of between 100–150 words in accordance with TEI guidelines. Students were instructed to use the TEI `said` element to enclose any instance of character speech, to identify the character whose speech is being introduced, and to classify each of these instances as either direct, indirect, or free indirect discourse and as either spoken aloud or thought silently. Because there are often several valid ways of interpreting a given passage, and because we are interested in how different students respond to the same passage, each 100–150 word span was assigned to three or four students. This first round of annotation focused only on the first four chapters of *TTL*. Raw average agreement of the various annotations at the level of the word was slightly less than 70%,[5] and though we hope to do better in our second round, levels of agreement typically required are likely to be beyond our reach due to the nature of the task. For example, all four sudents responsible for the passage cited above agreed on the tagging of the first two sentences; however, two students read the third sentence as FID mixing the voices of the narrator and Mrs. Ramsay, and two read it as FID mixing the voice of the narrator and James. Though they disagree, these are both valid interpretations of the passage.

In the second round of annotation, with 160 different student annotators assigned slightly longer spans of 200–300 words, we are focusing on the final seven chapters of *TTL*. We have made several minor changes to our annotation guidelines, and two significant changes. First, we now ask that in every span of text which students identify as FID, they explicitly identify the words that they regard as clearly coming from the subjective perspective of the character. We believe this will help students make a valid, defensible annotation, and it may also help with the computational analysis to follow. Second, we are also allowing embedded tags, for instances of direct or indirect discourse within spans of FID, which were confusing to students in the initial round. For instance, students would now be able to tag the above-cited passage of as a span of FID mixing the narrator's and Mrs. Ramsay's words, inside of which Mrs. Ramsay introduces an indirect-discourse rendering of her son's thoughts. Moving from a flat to a recursive representation will naturally result in additional complexity, but we believe it is necessary to capture what is happening in the text.

Once this second round of tagging is complete, we will begin our computational analysis. The aim is to see whether we can use supervised machine learning to replicate the way that second-year students enrolled in a rigorous English literature program respond to a highly complex text such as *TTL*. We are interested to see whether the subjective, messy data of the students can be used to train a useful model, even if it is inadequate as a gold standard. If successful, this algorithm could be deployed on the remaining, untagged sections of *TTL* (i.e. everything between the first four and last seven chapters) and produce meaningful readings of the text. It would proceed by (a) identifying passages of FID (that is, passages in which it is unclear whether a particular word belongs to the narrator or a character); (b) making an interpretation of that passage (hypothesizing as to which particular voices are being mixed); and (c) judging the likely validity of this interpretation. It would seek not only to *identify* spans of vocal ambiguity, but also to *describe* them, as far as possible. It would thus not aim strictly at disambiguation—at producing a right-or-wrong

[5] Since each passage was tagged by a different set of students, we cannot apply traditional kappa measures. Raw agreement overestimates success, since unlike kappa it does not discount random agreement, which in this case varies widely across the different kinds of annotation.

reading of the text—but rather at producing the best possible interpretation. The readings thus generated could then be reviewed by an independent expert as a form of evaluation.

Finally, we will develop an interactive website for the project. It will describe the background and aims of the project, present the results from the first three stages of the project, and also include an interface allowing visitors to the site to annotate the text for the same features as the students (via a Javascript interface, i.e. without having to manipulate the XML markup directly). This will provide further annotation data for our project, as well as giving instructors in English Literature and Digital Humanities a resource to use in their teaching.

5 Discussion

We believe our approach has numerous benefits on both sides of the divide. From a research perspective, the inter-disciplinary approach forces participants from both English Literature and Computational Linguistics to reconsider some of their fundamental disciplinary assumptions. The project takes humanities literary scholarship out of its "comfort zone" by introducing alien and unfamiliar methodologies such as machine learning, as well as by its basic premise that FID—by definition, a moment of uncertainty where the question of who is speaking is unresolved—can be detected automatically. Even though many of these problems can be linked with classic Computational Linguistics research areas, the project likewise takes Computational Linguistics out of its comfort zone by seeking not to resolve ambiguity but rather to identify it and, as far as possible, describe it. It presents an opportunity for a computational approach to take into account a primary insight of twentieth-century literary scholarship: that ambiguity and subjectivity are often desirable, intentional qualities of literary language, not problems to be solved. It promises literary scholarship a method for extending time-consuming, laborious human literary readings very rapidly to a vast number of literary texts, the possible applications of which are unclear at this early stage, but are surely great.

While many current major projects in computer-assisted literary analysis operate on a "big-data" model, drawing conclusions from analysis of vast numbers of lightly annotated texts, we see advantages in our own method of beginning with a few heavily-annotated texts and working outward. Traditional literary scholars often object that "big-data" readings take little or no account of subjective, human responses to literary texts; likewise, they find the broad conclusions of such projects (that the nineteenth century novel moves from telling to showing (Heuser and Le-Khac, 2012); that Austen is more influential than Dickens (Jockers, 2012)) difficult to test (or reconcile) with traditional literary scholarship. The specific method we are pursuing—taking a great number of individual human readings of a complex literary text and using them as the basis for developing a general understanding of how FID works—promises to move literary analysis beyond merely "subjective" readings without, however, denying the basis of all literary reading in individual, subjective responses. Our method indeed approaches the condition of a multi-voiced modernist literary work like *TTL*, in which, as Erich Auerbach perceived, "overlapping, complementing, and contradiction yield something that we might call a synthesized cosmic view". We too are building our synthetic understanding out of the diverse, often contradictory, responses of individual human readers.

Developing this project in an educational context—basing our project on readings developed by students as part of marked assignments for "The Digital Text"—is likewise beneficial to both cultures. It forces humanities undergraduates out of their comfort zone by asking them to turn their individual close readings of the text into an explicit, machine-readable representation (in this case, XML). Recognizing the importance of a sharable language for expressing literary features in machine-readable way, we have employed the standard TEI guidelines mark-up with as few customizations as possible, rather than developing our own annotation language from the ground up. The assignment asks students, however, to reflect critically on whether such explicit languages can ever adequately capture the polyvalent structures of meaning in literary texts; that is, whether there will always necessarily be possibilities that can't be captured in the tag set, and whether, as such, an algorithmic process can ever really "read" literature in a useful way. At the same time, this method has potentially great benefits to the development of such algorithmic readings, precisely by making available machine-readable approximations of how readers belonging to another "culture"—humanities undergraduates– respond to a challenging literary text. Such annotations would not be possible from a pool of annotators trained in the sciences, but could only come from students of the humanities with a basic understanding of XML. We do not believe, for example, workers on Amazon Mechanical Turk could reliably be used for this purpose, though it might be interesting to compare our 'studentsourcing' with traditional crowdsourcing techniques.

Our approach also faces several important challenges. Certainly the largest is whether an algorithmic criticism can be developed that could come to terms with ambiguity. The discipline of literary studies has long taught its students to accept what the poet John Keats called "negative capability, that is, when a man is capable of being in uncertainties, mysteries, doubts, without any irritable searching after fact and reason" (Keats, 2002). Computational analysis may simply be too fundamentally premised on "irritable searching after fact and reason" to be capable of "existing in uncertainty" in the manner of many human literary readers. Even if we are able to develop a successful algorithmic method of detecting FID in Woolf, this method may not prove applicable to other literary texts, which may employ the device in highly individual manners; *TTL* may prove simply too complex—and employ too much FID—to serve as a representative sample text. At a more practical level, even trained literature students do not produce perfect annotations: they make errors both in XML syntax and in their literary interpretation of *TTL*, a text that proves elusive even for some specialists. Since we do not want our algorithm to base its readings on invalid student readings (for instance, readings that attribute speech to a character clearly not involved in the scene), we face the challenge of weeding out bad student readings—and we will face the same challenge once readings begin to be submitted by visitors to the website. These diverse readings do, however, also present an interesting possibility, which we did not originally foresee: the development of a reader-response "map" showing how human readers actually interpret (and in many cases misinterpret) complex modernist texts like *TTL*.

6 Conclusion

Despite the philosophical and technical challenges that face researchers in this growing multidisciplinary area, we are increasingly optimistic that collaboration between computational and literary researchers is not only possible, but highly desirable. Interesting phenomena such as FID, this surprising melding of objective and personal perspective that is the subject of the current project, requires experts in both fields working together to identify, annotate, and ultimately model. Though fully resolving the rift between our two cultures is not, perhaps, a feasible goal, we argue that even this early and tentative collaboration has demonstrated the potential benefits on both sides.

Acknowledgements

This work was financially supported by the Social Sciences and Humanities Research Council of Canada and the Natural Sciences and Engineering Research Council of Canada.

References

M. H. Abrams. 1999. *A Glossary of Literary Terms*. Harcourt Brace, Toronto, 7th edition.

Cecilia Ovesdotter Alm. 2011. Subjective natural language problems: Motivations, applications, characterizations, and implications. In *Proceedings of the 49th Annual Meeting of the Association for Computational Linguistics: Human Language Technologies*, pages 107–112.

Shlomo Argamon, Casey Whitelaw, Paul Chase, Sobhan Raj Hota, Navendu Garg, and Shlomo Levitan. 2007. Stylistic text classification using functional lexical features. *Journal of the American Society for Information Science and Technology*, 7:91–109.

Erich Auerbach. 1953. *Mimesis: The Representation of Reality in Western Literature*. Princeton University Press, Princeton, NJ.

Mikhail Mikhailovich Bakhtin. 1981. Discourse in the novel. In Michael Holquist, editor, *The Dialogic Imagination: Four Essays*, pages 259–422. Austin: Univeristy of Texas Press.

Julian Brooke, Tong Wang, and Graeme Hirst. 2010. Automatic acquisition of lexical formality. In *Proceed-*

ings of the 23rd International Conference on Computational Linguistics (COLING '10), Beijing.

Julian Brooke, Adam Hammond, and Graeme Hirst. 2012. Unsupervised stylistic segmentation of poetry with change curves and extrinsic features. In *Proceedings of the 1st Workshop on Computational Literature for Literature (CLFL '12)*, Montreal.

Julian Brooke, Graeme Hirst, and Adam Hammond. 2013. Clustering voices in *the Waste Land*. In *Proceedings of the 2nd Workshop on Computational Literature for Literature (CLFL '13)*, Atlanta.

Cleanth Brooks. 1947. *The Well Wrought Urn*. Harcourt Brace, New York.

Barbara Di Eugenio and Michael Glass. 2004. The kappa statistic: a second look. *Computational Linguistics*, 30(1):95–101, March.

T.S. Eliot. 1971. The Waste Land. In *The Complete Poems and Plays, 1909–1950*, pages 37–55. Harcourt Brace Jovanovich, New York.

William Empson. 1930. *Seven Types of Ambiguity*. Chatto and Windus, London.

Julia Flanders. 2009. Data and wisdom: Electronic editing and the quantification of knowledge. *Literary and Linguistic Computing*, 24(1):53–62.

Amy Friedlander. 2009. Asking questions and building a research agenda for digital scholarship. Working Together or Apart: Promoting the Next Generation of Digital Scholarship. Report of a Workshop Cosponsored by the Council on Library and Information Resources and The National Endowment for the Humanities, March.

Adam Hammond. 2013. He do the police in different voices: Looking for voices in *The Waste Land*. Seminar: "Mapping the Fictional Voice" American Comparative Literature Association (ACLA).

Ryan Heuser and Long Le-Khac. 2012. A quantitative literary history of 2,958 nineteenth-century British novels: The semantic cohort method. Stanford Literary Lab Pamphlet No. 4. http://litlab.stanford.edu/LiteraryLabPamphlet4.pdf .

Susan Hockey. 2004. The history of humanities computing. In Ray Siemens, Susan Schreibman, and John Unsworth, editors, *A Companion to Digital Humanities*. Blackwell, Oxford.

David L. Hoover. 2007. Quantitative analysis and literary studies. In Ray Siemens and Susan Schreibman, editors, *A Companion to Digital Literary Studies*. Blackwell, Oxford.

Matthew L. Jockers. 2012. Computing and visualizing the 19th-century literary genome. Presented at the Digital Humanities Conference. Hamburg.

John Keats. 2002. *Selected Letters*. Oxford University Press, Oxford.

Xuan Le, Ian Lancashire, Graeme Hirst, and Regina Jokel. 2011. Longitudinal detection of dementia through lexical and syntactic changes in writing: A case study of three British novelists. *Literary and Linguistic Computing*, 26(4):435–461.

Kim Luyckx, Walter Daelemans, and Edward Vanhoutte. 2006. Stylogenetics: Clustering-based stylistic analysis of literary corpora. In *Proceedings of the 5th International Conference on Language Resources and Evaluation (LREC '06)*, Genoa, Italy.

Inderjeet Mani. 2013. *Computational Modeling of Narrative*. Morgan & Claypool.

Willard McCarty. 2005. *Humanities Computing*. Palgrave Macmillan, New York.

Jane Morris and Graeme Hirst. 2005. The subjectivity of lexical cohesion in text. In James G. Shanahan, Yan Qu, and Janyce M. Wiebe, editors, *Computing Attitude and Affect in Text*. Springer, Dordrecht, The Netherlands.

Stephen Ramsay. 2007. Algorithmic criticism. In Ray Siemens and Susan Schreibman, editors, *A Companion to Digital Literary Studies*. Blackwell, Oxford.

Ray Siemens, Susan Schreibman, and John Unsworth, editors. 2004. *A Companion to Digital Humanities*. Blackwell, Oxford.

C. P. Snow. 1959. *The Two Cultures and the Scientific Revolution*. Cambridge University Press, New York.

Maite Taboada, Julian Brooke, Milan Tofiloski, Kimberly Voll, and Manfred Stede. 2011. Lexicon-based methods for sentiment analysis. *Computational Linguistics*, 37(2):267–307.

Michael Toolan. 2008. Narrative progression in the short story: First steps in a corpus stylistic approach. *Narrative*, 16(2):105–120.

Byron Wallace. 2012. Multiple narrative disentanglement: Unraveling *Infinite Jest*. In *Proceedings of the 2012 Conference of the North American Chapter of the Association for Computational Linguistics: Human Language Technologies*, pages 1–10, Montréal, Canada, June. Association for Computational Linguistics.

Theresa Wilson, Janyce Wiebe, and Paul Hoffmann. 2005. Recognizing contextual polarity in phrase-level sentiment analysis. In *Proceedings of the conference on Human Language Technology and Empirical Methods in Natural Language Processing*, HLT/EMNLP '05, pages 347–354.

Virginia Woolf. 1927. *To the Lighthouse*. Hogarth, London.

Recognition of Classical Arabic Poems

Abdulrahman Almuhareb **Ibrahim Alkharashi** **Lama AL Saud** **Haya Altuwaijri**
Computer Research Institute
KACST
Riyadh, Saudi Arabia
{muhareb, kharashi, lalsaud, htuwaijri}@kacst.edu.sa

Abstract

This work presents a novel method for recognizing and extracting classical Arabic poems found in textual sources. The method utilizes the basic classical Arabic poem features such as structure, rhyme, writing style, and word usage. The proposed method achieves a precision of 96.94% while keeping a high recall value at 92.24%. The method was also used to build a prototype search engine for classical Arabic poems.

1 Introduction

Searching for poetry instances on the web, as well as identifying and extracting them, is a challenging problem. Contributing to the difficulty are the following: creators of web content do not usually follow a fixed standard format when publishing poetry content; there is no special HTML tags that can be used to identify and format poetry content; and finally poetry content is usually intermixed with other content published on the web.

In this paper, a classical Arabic poetry recognition and extraction method has been proposed. The method utilizes poem features and writing styles to identify and isolate one or more poem text bodies in a given piece of text. As an implementation of the poetry recognition and extraction method, a prototype Arabic poetry search engine was developed.

The paper is organized as follows. In Section 2, the related works are briefly discussed. Section 3 gives a general overview of Arabic poems features. Section 4 discusses the methodology used to identify and extract poem content from a given text. It also presents the used evaluation method. In Section 5, we discuss the experimentation including the used dataset and results. A prototype implementation of the method is presented in Section 6 followed by conclusions and future work plans.

2 Related Work

To the best of our knowledge, this work[1] is the first attempt to explore the possibility for building an automated system for recognizing and extracting Arabic poems from a given piece of text. The most similar work related to this effort is the work that has been done independently by Tizhoosh and Dara (2006) and Tizhoosh et al. (2008). The objective of Tizhoosh and his colleagues was to define a method that can distinguish between poem and non-poem (prose) documents using text classification techniques such as naïve Bayes, decision trees, and neural networks. The classifiers were applied on poetic features such as rhyme, shape, rhythm, meter, and meaning.

Another related work is by Al-Zahrani and Elshafei (2010) who filed a patent application for inventing a system for Arabic poetry meter identification. Their invention is based on Al-khalil bin Ahmed theory on Arabic poetry meters from the 8th century. The invented system accepts spoken or written Arabic poems to identify and verify their poetic meters. The system also can be used to assist the user in interactively producing poems based on a chosen meter.

Work on poem processing has been also conducted on other topics such as poem style and meter classification, rhyme matching, poem generation and quality evaluation. For example, Yi

1 Parts of this work are also presented in Patent Application No.: US 2012/0290602 A1.

et al. (2004) used a technique based on term connection for poetry stylistics analysis. He et al. (2007) used Support Vector Machines to differentiate bold-and-unconstrained styles from graceful-and-restrained styles of poetry. Hamidi et al. (2009) proposed a meter classification system for Persian poems based on features that are extracted from uttered poems. Reddy and Knight (2011) proposed a language-independent method for rhyme scheme identification. Manurung (2004) and Netzer et al. (2009) proposed two poem generation methods using hill-climbing search and word associations norms, respectively. In a recent work, Kao and Jurafsky (2012) proposed a method to evaluate poem quality for contemporary English poetry. Their proposed method computes 16 features that describe poem style, imagery, and sentiment. Kao and Jurafsky's result showed that referencing concrete objects is the primary indicator for professional poetry.

3 Features of Classical Arabic Poems

Traditionally, Arabic poems have been used as a medium for recording historical events, transferring messages among tribes, glorifying tribe or oneself, or satirizing enemies. Classical Arabic poems are characterized by many features. Some of these features are common to poems written in other languages, and some are specific to Arabic poems. Features of classical Arabic poems have been established in the pre-Islamic era and remained almost unchanged until now. Variation for such features can be noticed in contemporary (Paoli, 2001) and Bedouin (Palva, 1993) poems. In this section, we describe the Arabic poetic features that have been utilized in this work.

3.1 Presence

Instances of classical Arabic poems, as well as other types of poems, can be found in all sorts of printed and electronic documents including books, newspapers, magazines, and websites. An instance of classical Arabic poems can represent a complete poem or a poem portion. A single document can contain several classical Arabic poem instances. Poems can occur in designated documents by themselves or intermixed with normal text. In addition, poems can be found in non-textual media including audios, videos and images.

In the web, Arabic poem instances can be found in designated websites[2]. Only-poem websites normally organize poems in categories and adapt a unified style format that is maintained for the entire website. Hence, poem instances found in such websites are almost carefully written and should contain fewer errors. However, instances found in other websites such as forums and blogs are written in all sorts of styles and may contain mistakes in the content, spelling, and formatting.

3.2 Structure

Classical Arabic poems are written as a set of verses. There is no limit on the number of verses in a poem. However, a typical poem contains between twenty and a hundred verses (Maling, 1973). Arabic poem verses are short in length, compared to lines in normal text, and of equivalent length. Each verse is divided into two halves called hemistiches which also are equivalent in length.

3.3 Meter

The meters of classical Arabic poetry were modeled by Al-Khalil bin Ahmed in the 8th century. Al-Khalil's system consists of 15 meters (Al-Akhfash, a student of Al-Khalil, added the 16th meter later). Each meter is described by an ordered set of consonants and vowels. Most classical Arabic poems can be encoded using these identified meters and those that can't be encoded are considered unmetrical. Meters' patterns are applied on the hemistich level and each hemistich in the same poem must follow the same meter.

3.4 Rhyme

Classical Arabic poems follow a very strict but simple rhyme model. In this model, the last letter of each verse in a given poem must be the same. If the last letter in the verse is a vowel, then the second last letter of each verse must be the same as well. There are three basic vowel sounds in Arabic. Each vowel sound has two versions: a long and a short version. Short vowels are written as diacritical marks below or above the letter that precedes them while long vowels are written as whole letters. The two versions of each basic vowel are considered equivalent for rhyme purposes. Table 1

2 adab.com is an example for a dedicated website for Arabic poetry.

shows these vowel sets and other equivalent letters. These simple matching rules make rhyme detection in Arabic a much simpler task compared to English where different sets of letter combinations can signal the same rhyme (Tizhoosh & Dara 2006). On the other hand, the fact that, in modern Arabic writing, short vowels are ignored adds more challenges for the rhyme identification process. However, in poetry typesetting, typists tend not to omit short vowels especially for poems written in standard Arabic.

Table 1: Equivalent vowels and letters

Equivalent Vowels		**Equivalent Letters**	
/a/, /a:/	ا، ى، َ	*ta, ta marbutah*	ت، ة
/u/, /u:/	و، وا، ُ	*ha, ta marbutah*	ه، ة
/i/, /i:/	ي، ِ		

Verse 1	**H1**	يقضون بالأمر عنها وهي غافلة
	H2	ما دار في فلك منها وفي قُطُبِ
Verse 2	**H1**	لو بيَّنت قطّ أمراً قبل موقعه
	H2	لم تُخْفِ ماحلّ بالأوثان والصلُبِ
Verse 3	**H1**	فَتْحُ الفُتوحِ تَعَالَى أَنْ يُحيطَ بِهِ
	H2	نَظْمٌ مِن الشعْرِ أَوْ نَثْرٌ مِنَ الخُطَبِ
Verse 4	**H1**	فتحٌ تفتَّحُ أبوابُ السَّماءِ لهُ
	H2	وتبرزُ الأرضُ في أثوابها القُشُبِ

Figure 1: An example of classical Arabic poems with four verses written in Style 1. H1 and H2 are the first and second hemistich.

3.5 Writing Styles

There are three predominant writing styles of classical Arabic poems: (1) the poem is written in a single column with each verse in two rows; (2) the poem is written in a single column with each verse in two rows where the first half of each verse is written aligned to the right and the second half of each verse is aligned to the left; and (3) the poem is written such that each verse is written as two halves on the same row and separated by one or more punctuation marks or spaces. In some cases, this style can also be written without any separators and the end of the first half and the start of the second half have to be guessed by the reader. Figures 1 to 3 show examples of the three writing styles of classical Arabic poems.

Verse 1	**H1**	يقضون بالأمر عنها وهي غافلة
	H2	ما دار في فلك منها وفي قُطُبِ
Verse 2	**H1**	لو بيَّنت قطّ أمراً قبل موقعه
	H2	لم تُخْفِ ماحلّ بالأوثان والصلُبِ
Verse 3	**H1**	فَتْحُ الفُتوحِ تَعَالَى أَنْ يُحيطَ بِهِ
	H2	نَظْمٌ مِن الشعْرِ أَوْ نَثْرٌ مِنَ الخُطَبِ
Verse 4	**H1**	فتحٌ تفتَّحُ أبوابُ السَّماءِ لهُ
	H2	وتبرزُ الأرضُ في أثوابها القُشُبِ

Figure 2: An example of classical Arabic poems with four verses written in Style 2.

	Hemistich 2		**Hemistich 1**
Verse 1	ما دار في فلك منــــها وفي قُطُـــبِ	**	يقضون بالأمر عنها وهي غافلة
Verse 2	لم تُخْفِ ماحلّ بالأوثان والصلُـــبِ	**	لو بيَّنت قطّ أمراً قـــبل موقعـــه
Verse 3	نَظْمٌ مِن الشعْرِ أَوْ نَثْرٌ مِنَ الخُطَبِ	**	فَتْحُ الفُتوحِ تَعَالَى أَنْ يُحيـــطَ بِهِ
Verse 4	وتبرزُ الأرضُ في أثوابها القُشُـــبِ	**	فتحٌ تفتَّحُ أبـــوابُ السَّمـــاءِ لـــهُ

Figure 3: An example of classical Arabic poems with four verses written in Style 3.

3.6 Word Usage

It is very noticeable that classical Arabic poets tend not to use words repetitively in a given poem. To evaluate this observation, we analyzed a random set of 134 poem instances. We found duplicate start words (excluding common stop words) in 22% of the poems. Duplicate end words were found in 31% of the poems. However, the probability of encountering a verse with a duplicate start in the same poem is only 3% and 4% for a duplicate end word.

4 Method

The proposed method for standard Arabic poem recognition utilizes the poetic features described previously including structure, rhyme, writing style, and word usage. The meter feature was not literally used in the proposed method and may be used in a future work. The system operation is summarized by the flowchart shown in Figure 5 and described by the following steps:

1. Read input text line by line accepting only lines with reasonable size (e.g., lines of size between 2 and 20 words).
2. Collect consecutive lines that have equivalent length: compute the length of the line by counting the characters in the line. Lines are considered equivalent in length if the length difference is below a certain threshold (e.g., 40%, as has been used in the experiment discussed below).
3. Identify lines with separators to process Style 3 candidate verses. Separators are identified by searching for a set of white spaces or punctuations in the middle of the line between two halves. If identified, transform Style 3 to Style 1 shape for normalization.
4. Identify candidate rhymes at the end of each line.
5. Identify poems: searching for candidate poems in a consecutive list of candidate half-verses can produce several solutions based on rhyme. Select solution that produces poems with the maximum possible lengths. Figure 4 shows an example for a multiple solution case.
6. Repeat steps 1 to 5 until the end of the text body is reached.

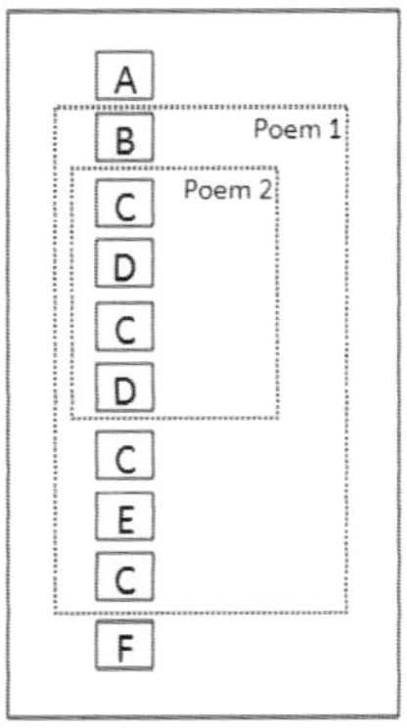

Figure 4: An example for multiple solutions based on rhyme. A list of 10 candidate half-verses indicated by their rhymes from A to F. Poem 1 starts at line 2 and ends at line 9 with 4 verses and rhyme C. Poem 2 starts at line 3 and ends at line 6 with 2 verses and rhyme D. The proposed method will select Poem 1 instead of Poem 2 since it has more verses.

Following these steps, the proposed method can recognize instances of classical Arabic poems of size at least two verses in any plain text. Detecting instances of a single verse is not covered in this work because the recognition process is only triggered by repetitive patterns that can't occur within single verse instances.

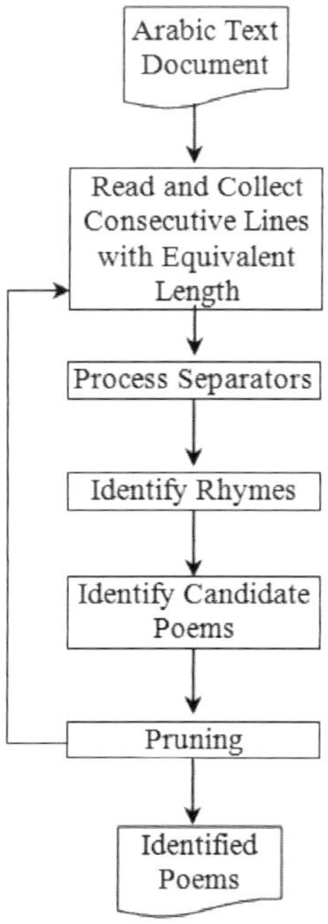

Figure 5: A flowchart of the proposed system for Arabic poems recognition.

4.1 Handling ill-formed cases

The proposed method can be applied on plain text from any source regardless of formatting and typing quality. Common formatting and typing mistakes and ambiguity are resolved as follows:

1. Mismatched and false separators: Mismatched separators occur when a set of candidate verses share the same rhyme but with different verse separators. Here, we treat the separators as if they were similar assuming that the separators were incorrectly typed. False separators, on the other hand, is identified when a set of candidate verses share the same rhyme and one or more verses were identified as having separators and the remaining verses have not. In this case, we ignore the identified separators assuming that these misidentified separators are just normal punctuation

marks. Figure 6 and 7 show real examples from the web for mismatched and false separators, respectively.

هذا الذي تعرف البطحاء وطاته **** والبيت يعرفه والحل والحرم

هذا ابن خير عباد الله كلهم **** هذا التقي النقي الطاهر العلم

اذا راته قريش قال قائلها *** الي مكارم هذا ينتهي الكرم

ينمي الي ذروة العز التي قصرت ** عن نيلها عرب الاسلام والعجم

Figure 6: An example of mismatched separators for a poem instance with four verses that share the same rhyme. The first two verses share the same separator while the third and the forth verses have similar but not exact separators.

مايقول الشعر .. من باله خلي

ومن نساه الهم لايطري القصيد

ماكتبت الشعر قصدي تزعلي

وان فرحتي فيه ما اقصد اكيد

حس يشعرني .. وضيقة تنجلي

ودار تسكني وانا عنها بعيد

Figure 7: An example of false separators for a poem instance with three verses that share the same rhyme. The first half of the first and third verses contain dots (..) at the middle of the line which can mistakenly be identified as separators.

2. Absence of short vowels: To treat missing short vowels in rhyme, we, recursively, assume the existence of the vowel if missing in a given verse and exists in a neighboring verse. Here, the last character in the former verse must match the second last character in the neighboring verse. Figure 8 shows an example of this case.

كالزهر في ترفٍ والبدر في شرفٍ *** و البحر في كرمٍ و الدهر في همم

كأنه و هو فردٌ من جلالته *** في عسكر حين تلقاه و في حشم

كأنما اللؤلؤ المكنون فى صدفٍ *** من معدني منطق منه و مبتسم

لا طيب يعدل تُرباً ضم أعظمهُ *** طوبى لمنتشق منه و ملتثمِ

Figure 8: An example of short vowels absence for a poem instance with four verses. The first three verses neglect the short vowel *Kasrah* that exists at the end of the fourth verse.

3. Absence of separators: This case is triggered when encountering a set of consecutive lines sharing the same rhyme, and having line length in words that exceed half of the threshold for valid lines, and of course have no identifiable separators. The proposed remedy is to locate the closest whitespace to the center of each line and split the lines at those points and generate a verse of two hemistiches from each line. Figure 9 shows an example of this case.

مولاي صلي وسلم دائماً أبدا على حبيبك خير الخلق كلهم

أبان مولده عن طيب عنصره يا طيب مبتدأ منه ومختتم

يومٌ تفرّس فيه الفرس أنهم قد أنذروا بحلول البؤس والنقم

وبات إيوان كسرى وهو منصدعٌ كشمل أصحاب كسرى غير ملتئم

والنار خامدة الأنفاس من أسفٍ عليه والنهر ساهي العين من سدم

Figure 9: An example of absence of separators for a poem instance with five verses.

4.2 Pruning

Based on our observations during the development phase of the proposed method, it was noticeable that the robustness of the method correlates positively with the number of verses in the candidate poem. This is because with each additional verse the accumulated evidences are reconfirmed repetitively. This is not the case with few verses candidates. The probability of encountering a false matching rhyme for example with two or three verses is much higher. To resolve these cases and improve the precision of the proposed method, we introduce the following pruning tests to be applied only to short candidate poems:

1. Reject short candidate instances with low average number of words per half-verses. For example, using a threshold of 3 words.
2. Accept only short candidate instances that have at least two letters rhymes.
3. Reject short candidate instances when number of words per half-verse is not equivalent.
4. Reject short candidate instances with duplicate starting or ending words that exceed a threshold of 20%, for example.

4.3 Evaluation Measure

To evaluate the proposed method, we applied the F-measure (Swets, 1969) based on the precision and recall measures. Precision, as shown in Equation 1, is calculated by dividing the total number of the correct lines produced by the method over the total number of lines in the output. Given that our method processes the input data and generates output as half-verse per line. Recall, as shown in Equation 2, is computed similarly except that we divide over the model total number of correct lines. The model resembles the prefect solution for such input data.

$$Precision = \frac{System\ Total\ Number\ of\ Correct\ Lines}{System\ Total\ Number\ of\ Lines} \quad (1)$$

$$Recall = \frac{System\ Total\ Number\ of\ Correct\ Lines}{Model\ Total\ Number\ of\ Correct\ Lines} \quad (2)$$

5 Experiment

5.1 Dataset

During the development phase of the method, we used several development datasets utilizing data drawn from the web. For evaluation purposes, we assembled a dataset using text from hundred randomly selected HTML web-pages. The set contains 50 HTML pages with classical Arabic poem instances (positive set) and 50 pages without poem instances (negative set). To select the positive set, we randomly chose 5 poets and searched Google and selected the first 10 pages that contain poem instances for each poet. The negative set was similarly chosen by selecting the first 50 pages that contain no poem instances for an arbitrary query. Text from the selected web-pages was converted to plain text using the Apache Tika toolkit[3] and saved in a single large text file. This resulted in a text file that contains about 23K non-empty lines including 161 classical Arabic poem instances having 4,740 half-verses.

5.2 Result

The poem dataset was used to evaluate the proposed poem recognition method. Figure 10 shows the results using five different pruning levels. The levels indicate the minimum number of verses for the pruning tests to be applied. Level 0 shows the performance without applying any of the pruning tests. The remaining levels show the results when the pruning is applied on candidates with at most two, three, and four verses, respectively. Level 4* is similar to Level 4 but here the fourth pruning test (duplicate words test) is applied on every candidate instance instead of only candidates with at most four verses.

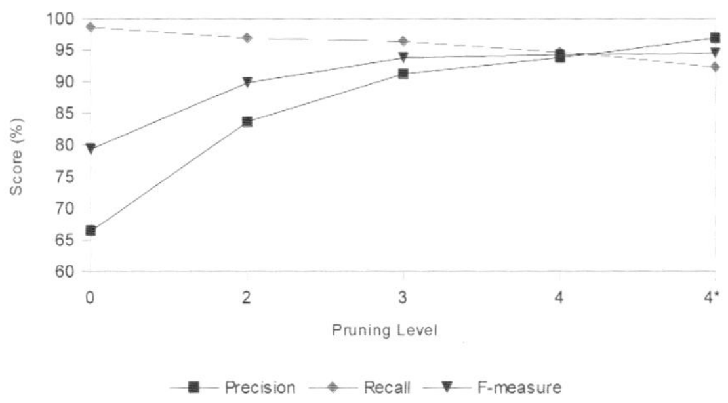

Figure 10: Evaluation results using five different pruning levels.

6 A Prototype Poem Search Engine

In order to assess the performance of the proposed poem recognition method in a real-life application, a prototype search engine for Arabic poems was implemented[4]. The search engine was built using the Apache Nutch web crawler and the Solr search engine to provide regular search engine services including crawling, parsing, and indexing. The HTML parsing plug-in in Nutch was extended using the proposed method to be able to recognize Arabic poems. Using this scenario, the search engine was successfully used to crawl a set of websites, identify all poem and non-poem instances, and index poem instances only. Figure 11 shows a snapshot of the search engine website.

3 The Apache Tika toolkit can be downloaded from http://tika.apache.org/

4 The Arabic poem prototype search engine can be accessed at http://naba.kacst.edu.sa

Figure 11: A snapshot of the prototype poem search engine

7 Conclusions and Future Work

In this paper, we proposed a method for classical Arabic poem recognition. The proposed method was able to identify Arabic poems in any unstructured text with a very high accuracy. The method utilizes the common features of classical Arabic poems such as structure, writing style, and rhyme; and employs them in the recognition process. A specialized search engine for classical Arabic poems was implemented as a prototype using the proposed method with promising results. For the future, we plan to enhance the method by introducing the well known meter model for classical Arabic poems. We would also like to extend the coverage of the method to include other types of Arabic poetry, namely contemporary Arabic. For the specialized search engine, we plan to add more features such as providing different search boundaries, for example, within a poem, a verse, or a hemistich. Moreover, we would like to find automatic ways to relate a poem to its poet.

Acknowledgments

The authors would like to thank Waleed Almutairi and Abdulelah Almubarak from KACST for their assistance in implementing the prototype poem search engine.

References

Al-Zahrani, A.K., Elshafei, M., 2010. Arabic poetry meter identification system and method. Patent Application US 2010/0185436.

Hamidi, S., Razzazi, F., Ghaemmaghami, M.P., 2009. Automatic Meter Classification in Persian Poetries Using Support Vector Machines. Presented at the IEEE International Symposium on Signal Processing and Information Technology (ISSPIT).

He, Z.-S., Liang, W.-T., Li, L.-Y., Tian, Y.-F., 2007. SVM-Based Classification Method for Poetry Style. Presented at the Sixth International Conference on Machine Learning and Cybernetics, Hong Kong.

Kao, J., Jurafsky, D., 2012. A Computational Analysis of Style, Affect, and Imagery in Contemporary Poetry, in: In Proceedings of the NAACL-HLT 2012 Workshop on Computational Linguistics for Literature. Montreal, Canada, pp. 8–17.

Maling, J., 1973. The theory of classical Arabic metrics (dissertation).

Manurung, H.M., 2004. An Evolutionary Algorithm Approach to Poetry Generation (PhD thesis).

Netzer, Y., Gabay, D., Goldberg, Y., Elhadad, M., 2009. Gaiku: Generating Haiku with Word Associations Norms. Presented at the Workshop on Computational Approaches to Linguistic Creativity (CALC '09).

Palva, H., 1993. Metrical problems of the contemporary Bedouin Qasida: A linguistic approach. Asian Folklore Studies 52, 75–92.

Paoli, B., 2001. Meters and Formulas: The Case of Ancient Arabic Poetry. Belgian Journal of Linguistics 15, 113–136.

Reddy, S., Knight, K., 2011. Unsupervised Discovery of Rhyme Schemes. Presented at the 49th Annual Meeting of the Association for Computational Linguistics, Portland, Oregon, pp. 77–82.

Swets, J.A., 1969. Effectiveness of information retrieval methods. American Documentation 20, 72–89.

Tizhoosh, H.R., Dara, R.A., 2006. On Poem Recognition. Pattern Analysis and Applications, Springer 9, 325–338.

Tizhoosh, H.R., Sahba, F., Dara, R., 2008. Poetic Features for Poem Recognition: A Comparative Study. Journal of Pattern Recognition Research 3.

Yi, Y., He, Z.-S., Li, L.-Y., Yu, T., 2004. Studies on Traditional Chinese Poetry Style Identification. Presented at the Third International Conference on Machine Learning and Cybernetics, Shanghai.

Tradition and Modernity in 20th Century Chinese Poetry

Rob Voigt
Center for East Asian Studies
Stanford University
robvoigt@stanford.edu

Dan Jurafsky
Linguistics Department
Stanford University
jurafsky@stanford.edu

Abstract

Scholars of Chinese literature note that China's tumultuous literary history in the 20th century centered around the uncomfortable tensions between tradition and modernity. In this corpus study, we develop and automatically extract three features to show that the classical character of Chinese poetry decreased across the century. We also find that Taiwan poets constitute a surprising exception to the trend, demonstrating an unusually strong connection to classical diction in their work as late as the '50s and '60s.

1 Introduction

For virtually all of Chinese history through the fall of the Qing Dynasty, poetry was largely written in Classical Chinese and accessible to a small, educated fraction of the population. With the rise of the May Fourth Movement in 1919, prominent intellectuals such as Hu Shi and Lu Xun began to advocate for and produce a fresh vernacular literature.

This upheaval of tradition has been much discussed in literary studies; Michelle Yeh calls vernacular poetry "a self-proclaimed iconoclast struggling against a formidable predecessor: the heritage of three millennia of classical poetry" (Yeh, 1991).

While some propose that the May Fourth intellectuals "abolished the classical language and all of its literary genres" (Hockx and Smits, 2003), others make more measured claims: Mao Chen, for example, maintains that "a special relationship to tradition informs all phases of cultural activity during the May Fourth period" (Chen, 1997).

Julia Lin notes that the period following the May Fourth Movement through 1937 saw "the most exciting and diverse experimentation in the history of modern Chinese poetry" (Lin, 1973). Much of this experimentation was concerned with the question of modernity versus tradition, wherein some poets "adapt[ed] the reality of the modern spoken language to what they felt was the essence of the old classical Chinese forms" (Haft, 1989).

The founding of the People's Republic of China in 1949 was a second major turning point in the century, when "the Communists in one cataclysmic sweep [...] ruthlessly altered the course of the arts" and poetry "became totally subservient to the dictates of the party" (Lin, 1973). With the "physical removal of the old cultural leadership," many of whom fled to Taiwan, this period saw a substantial "vacuum in literature and the arts" (McDougall and Louie, 1997).

Post-Mao, publication restrictions gradually loosened and earlier cultural journals re-entered circulation. Poetry began to reclaim its audience, and a Chinese avant-garde associated with the "Misty Poets" developed (McDougall and Louie, 1997).

However, we lack broad-scale empirical evidence of the linguistic features that constituted the shift from tradition to modernity. Therefore, we propose a study that asks: To what extent were classical poetic forms and classical language immediately discarded with the advent of vernacular poetry? What is the status of classical language after 1949 and amidst the Maoist era, when we might expect its total absence? Does more contemporary poetry still draw connections to classical language?

2 Prior Work on Chinese Poetry in NLP

The majority of existing studies in NLP on Chinese poetry deal exclusively with the classical language.

Jiang and Zhou (2008) explore the problem of classical Chinese poetic couplets, and to develop a system to generate them automatically using techniques from machine translation.

Fang et al. (2009) use an ontology of imagery developed by Lo (2008) to identify imagery in classical Chinese poems, and develop a parser that is able to extract tree structures that identify complex imagistic language in the same.

More recent work develops useful resources for understanding classical poetry. Lee (2012) develops a corpus of classical Chinese poems that are word-segmented and annotated with nested part-of-speech tags that allow for different interpretations of "wordhood" - a non-trivial concept in considering Chinese texts classical and modern. Lee and Kong (2012) introduce a large-scale dependency treebank annotated on a corpus of 8th-century poems.

To our knowledge, there is no existing computational work that attempts to understand the development of modern Chinese poetry over time.

3 Data Collection

For this project, we use a corpus of modern poems collected on the site "Chinese Poetry Treasury" (中国诗歌库, www.shigeku.com) entitled the "Selected Database of Chinese Modern Poetry" (中国现代诗歌精品资料库). It is important to note that the poems in this collection were hand-selected by the group running the site for their canonicity, so our data are biased towards those poems that have, in a sense, "stood the test of time" in the eyes of a mainland Chinese readership.

This corpus is distributed through their site as a collection of html documents, one page per poet, which include brief biographical information for the poet and a collection of their works. We use unix command-line tools (sed, tr, iconv, grep) and basic python scripting to process these documents into a usable corpus with each poem as a separate, clean file, segmented character-by-character. [1]

The site categorizes poets by their "most active" decade, from the 1920s through the 1990s, and we extract this metadata to allow for comparisons over time. In our analysis, however, a methodological impediment arose: namely, the Cultural Revolution.

As discussed in the introduction, this tumultuous period severely disrupted the developmental path of modern Chinese literature. Indeed, we find in our corpus that almost none of the poets tagged as active in the '50s and '60s were mainland Chinese, but instead Taiwanese poets who fled to the island at the climax of the Chinese Civil War.

For this reason, combined with the potential noisiness induced by the fact that decade tags are per-poet instead of per-poem, we manually identify Taiwan poets and divide our corpus into three subsets for analysis: "early modern" poetry in the 1920s and '30s; "late modern" poetry in the '40s interrupted by the Maoist era but resuming in the late '70s, '80s, and '90s; and "Taiwan" poetry by Taiwan natives and transplanted mainlanders in Taiwan post-1949.

After pre-processing, our full corpus for analysis (denoted *Eval* in Table 1) contains 3,611 poems by 305 poets, with a total of 1,128,428 Chinese characters. This size is large enough for meaningful computational results, but small enough to allow for significant qualitative analysis.

We will later define metrics for evaluating the "classicality" of individual characters and radicals, so we process auxiliary corpora (denoted *Aux* in Table 1) of classical poetry and contemporary prose. For classical Chinese, we use a large corpus, from the same source (www.shigeku.com), of poems from the Tang Dynasty (618-907 AD), often considered the greatest classical era for Chinese poetry. For modern Chinese, we use a subset of a machine translation bi-text, comprised primarily of contemporary newswire, legal, and other prose texts.[2]

Since we aim to discover the overall "classicality" of association for individual characters, our auxiliary corpora are cross-genre to exaggerate the effects — a high "classicality" score will indicate both a period-specific classicality and a classical poetic genre association.

[1] Scripts and further information are available here: http://nlp.stanford.edu/robvoigt/chpoetry/

[2] From the BOLT Phase 1 Evaluation training data; see http://www.nist.gov/itl/iad/mig/bolt_p1.cfm

Table 1: Corpus inventory.

		Poems	Chars	Vocab
Eval	Early	351	89,226	3,299
	Taiwan	513	126,369	3,878
	Late	2,747	912,833	4,852
Aux	Classical		2,712,685	6,263
	Modern		9,405,549	5,517

4 Methodology

Speak in the language of the time in which you live.

— Hu Shi, 1917

As suggested in the introduction, modern poetry is distinguished linguistically from classical poetry in its explicit shift to the use of vernacular language. Classical poetry is formalized, concise, and imagistic. We propose three features to operationalize this classicality and computationally observe the shift to a poetic vernacular across the 20th century.

Final Rhyme Classical Chinese poetry in general has a highly regular structure, following strict metrical and rhyming conventions, and most prominently employs a highly consistent end-rhyme. We use the CJKLIB python library[3] to obtain the pronunciation for the last character in each line of each poem. The pronunciation of a given Chinese character may be divided into precisely one consonant (known as an "initial") and one vowel (known as a "final").

We therefore qualify a given line as "rhyming" if the last character of any line within a 3-line window shares its vowel final pronunciation, and for each poem calculate the proportion of rhyming lines.

Character-based Probability Ratio Inspired by the work of Underwood and Sellers (2012) in tracking shifts in literary diction in English poetry, we use our auxiliary corpora of Tang Dynasty poems and modern Chinese language text to create two simple metrics for understanding the "classicality" of poetic diction.

The extreme concision of classical poetry "focuses attention on the characters themselves" (Hinton, 2010), with common classical forms containing as few as ten or twenty characters. To analyze classical diction, for each character we aim to get a ratio describing how classical it sounds.

[3]http://code.google.com/p/cjklib/

For this metric, we calculate the probability of each character occurring in its respective corpus using add-one smoothing. We then define the score for a given character as the difference of the character's log likelihood of occurring in the classical auxiliary corpus with its log likelihood of occurring in the modern auxiliary corpus. Scores range from -8 to +8, where a higher score indicates a more "classically"-tinged character.

We find these scores match up well with intuition. In the highly negative range, we find recently-invented, conversational, and grammatical characters unique to the modern vernacular. In the highly positive range, we find rareified literary, poetic characters. In the range surrounding 0.0, we find many common, persistent characters whose meanings have changed little over time. Selected examples of these scores can be seen in Table 2.

Table 2: Example classicality scores for selected characters on the Character-based Probability Ratio metric.

Character	Meaning	Score
	HIGHLY CLASSICAL	
遇 *yu*	To meet; to encounter	7.94
衾 *qin*	A thin quilt used to cover a corpse in a coffin	6.42
萧 *xiao*	A type of bamboo flute	5.99
柳 *liu*	Willow	4.68
	SIMILAR ACROSS PERIODS	
听 *ting*	Listen; hear	0.64
去 *qü*	To go; towards	0.61
直 *zhi*	Directly	-0.11
收 *shou*	To receive; to harvest	-0.53
	HIGHLY MODERN	
你 *ni*	Second-person pronoun	-4.49
够 *gou*	Sufficient; enough	-6.02
呢 *ne*	Sentence-final particle	-6.67
她 *ta*	Third-person female pronoun	-7.82

We calculate a score for a given poem on this metric by simply taking the average of the character-based probability ratio for each character in the poem. These results are denoted *Char* in Table 4.

Radical-based Probability Ratio This metric is fundamentally similar to the above character-based method, but offers the potential to provide a different kind of insight. The majority of Chinese characters are compositional, with a semantic component and a phonetic component.

We start from the intuition that contemporary texts will be more likely to use characters that contain the 口 (*kou*, "mouth") radical as their semantic component, because this radical is commonly found in modern conversational particles that were not used in ancient texts. We generalize this hypothesis and consider that the use of characters with certain semantic radicals is correlated with the classicality of a text.

We again use the CJKLIB python library to process our auxiliary corpora, extracting the semantic component radical from each character and calculating the ratio of its probability of occurrence, with add-one smoothing, in the auxiliary classical and modern corpora. As above, we obtain the ratio scores for each radical, and score each poem in our corpus by averaging these scores for each character in the poem.

While these scores are less immediately accessible to intuition than those of the character-based metric, the radical-based scores, with examples seen in Table 3, demonstrate a consistency that parallels the character-based scores.

The semantic radicals most prevalent in classical poetry include those signifying bird, horse, valley, mountain, ghost, dragon, and so on; classical poetry has a pastoral and mythological aesthetic that is directly reflected in the distribution of its radicals. Conversely, modern prose is more likely to use semantic radicals related to work, family, money, speech, and movement; they convey the practical realism of contemporary conversational speech.

Table 3: Example classicality scores for selected semantic radicals on the Radical-based Probability Ratio metric.

Radical	Meaning	Score
	HIGHLY CLASSICAL	
鬼 *gui*	Ghost	2.18
山 *shan*	Mountain	2.09
虫 *chong*	Insect	1.43
	SIMILAR ACROSS PERIODS	
女 *nü*	Female	0.01
文 *wen*	Culture; language	-0.02
生 *sheng*	Life; birth	-0.01
	HIGHLY MODERN	
手 *shou*	Hand	-0.48
言 *yan*	Words; speech	-0.61
力 *li*	Force; work	-0.94

4.1 Diachronic Statistical Analysis

We began from the hypothesis that each of the metrics described above will demonstrate, broadly, that the classical nature of Chinese poetry decreased over the course of the 20th century. The raw statistical counts for our features can been seen in Table 4.

Table 4: Raw feature statistics across sub-corpora. Higher values in the AVG rows indicate a greater "classicality." For all three features, classicality decreased over the century, with the exception of Taiwan.

		Early	Taiwan	Late
Rhyme	AVG	0.281	0.244	0.226
	STDDEV	0.193	0.169	0.152
Char	AVG	-0.695	-0.620	-0.882
	STDDEV	0.494	0.446	0.404
Radical	AVG	-0.072	-0.081	-0.116
	STDDEV	0.121	0.105	0.097

We calculate the presence of the "classical" features defined above for each subset, and compute a binary logistic regression with the scikit-learn python library (Pedregosa et al., 2011)[4] to find correlation coefficients for those features between the "early modern" and "late modern" subsets.

5 Results and Discussion

Several claims from the literary community are well-supported by our results.

Logistic regression reveals a significant downward trend for our features as we shift from "early modern" to "late modern" poetry ($R^2 = 0.89$), indicating decreased use of end-rhyme, increased use of modern characters, and increased prevalence of modern semantic radicals over the course of the century.

Though the early works use more classical characters on the whole, we also observe a higher statistical variance for all metrics in the '20s and '30s, supporting the literary hypothesis that the May Fourth period was one of increased experimentation that later settled into a somewhat more consistent modernity.

We find, however, less support for the idea that Chinese modern poets "abolished the classical language" in their work (Hockx and Smits, 2003).

[4]http://scikit-learn.org

Throughout the century we find repeated instances of highly classical language, with individual poems reaching a maximum character-based probability ratio of 0.70 in the "early" works, 0.76 in the "late" works, and 0.87 in the "Taiwan" works; compare these with an average score of 1.20 for the auxiliary classical dataset overall. Considering that a score of 0.0 would indicate an equal distribution of weight between "classical" and "modern" characters, it's clear that these 20th-century poems still contain a substantial proportion of characters drawn from the classical language.

Poems from Taiwan in the '50s and '60s offer perhaps the most interesting results in this study. It's notable in the first place that poets in our corpus selected as worth remembering by contemporary mainland Chinese from the most authoritarian period of Communist control are almost exclusively from Taiwanese authors. Furthermore, the dip towards modernity we see in '40s mainland poetry was rejected in the next decade by those mainland poets who found themselves in Taiwan after 1949; the Taiwan poems bear far greater resemblance to the early subset of our data than to the late.

This finding parallels work on this period from literary scholars. Yvonne Chang writes that in '50s and '60s Taiwan, valorization of traditional Chinese culture and romanticization of the early 20th-century Nationalist period in mainland China was heavily encouraged. In particular, the concept of "纯文学" (*chun wenxue*, "pure literature") gained popularity in Taiwan's literary circles, and with it came a resurgence of more traditional diction and forms (Chang, 1993).

Fangming Chen further describes poetry in postwar Taiwan as a political outlet for the Kuomintang, the sole ruling party of Taiwan at the time, as they "forcefully brought Chinese nationalism" to the island. Poets who demonstrated a deep "nostalgia" for the "motherland" of mainland China were far more likely to be rewarded with cultural resources such as grants and publication money, being that the government had a vested interest in keeping the public on board with plans to "reclaim the homeland" (Chen, 2007). It is fascinating, then, that we observe this tendency computationally with a return to the levels of classicality seen in '20s and '30s mainland China.

In spite of these encouraging results, this work has several limitations. Our reliance on decade-based labels applied to poets, rather than poems, introduces significant noise. The outlier behavior observed in Taiwan poets is indicative of the need for a better understanding of regional differences, and a comparison with a similarly isolated Sinophone region such as Hong Kong would be productive in this regard. In both cases, information extraction techniques might allow us to tag poems with their date of publication and poets with their hometown, facilitating fine-grained analysis, as would a broader dataset that goes beyond the modern canon.

6 Conclusion

In this paper, we computationally operationalized three features that successfully track the declining influence of classical poetic style and language in 20th-century Chinese poetry. We identified Taiwan poets as an outlier in the dataset, and found empirical evidence for the political externalities of the '50s and '60s that called for a return to a nostalgic classicism. In this way, this work presents a promising first step to a thorough empirical understanding of the development of modern Chinese poetry.

Acknowledgments

Thanks to three anonymous reviewers for detailed and insightful comments. This research was supported in part by the Foreign Language and Area Studies Fellowships, United States Department of Education.

References

Sung-sheng Yvonne Chang. 1993. *Modernism and the Nativist Resistance*. Duke University Press: Durham and London.

Fangming Chen. 2007. Postmodern or Postcolonial? An Inquiry into Postwar Taiwanese Literary History. In *Writing Taiwan*, David Der-wei Wang and Carlos Rojas, eds. Duke University Press, Durham and London.

Mao Chen. 1997. *Between Tradition and Change*. University Press of America, Lanham, MA.

Alex Chengyu Fang, Fengju Lo, and Cheuk Kit Chinn. 2009. Adapting NLP and Corpus Analysis Techniques to Structured Imagery Analysis in Classical Chinese Poetry. In *Workshop Adaptation of Language Resources and Technology to New Domains*, Borovets, Bulgaria.

Lloyd Haft. 1989. *A Selective Guide to Chinese Literature: 1900-1949*. E.J. Brill, New York.

David Hinton, ed. 2010. *Classical Chinese Poetry: An Anthology*. Farrar, Straus, and Giroux.

Michel Hockx and Ivo Smits, eds. 2003. *Reading East Asian Writing: The Limits of Literary Theory*. RoutledgeCurzon, London and New York.

Long Jiang and Ming Zhou. 2008. Generating Chinese Couplets using a Statistical MT Approach. In *COLING*.

John Lee. 2012. A Classical Chinese Corpus with Nested Part-of-Speech Tags. In *Proceedings of the 6th EACL Workshop on Language Technology for Cultural Heritage, Social Sciences, and Humanities*, Avignon, France.

John Lee and Yin Hei Kong. 2012. A Dependency Treebank of Classical Chinese Poems. In *NAACL-HLT*, Montreal, Canada.

Julia Lin. 1973. *Modern Chinese Poetry: An Introduction*. University of Washington Press, Seattle, WA.

Fengju Lo. 2008. The Research of Building a Semantic Cetegory System Based on the Language Characteristic of Chinese Poetry. In *Proceedings of the 9th Cross-Strait Symposium on Library Information Science*.

Lu Zhiwei. 1984. *Five Lectures on Chinese Poetry*. Joint Publishing Co., Hong Kong.

Bonnie McDougall and Kam Louie, eds. 1997. *The Literature of China in the Twentieth Century*. Hurst and Company, London.

Fabian Pedregosa, Gaël Varoquaux, Alexandre Gramfort, Vincent Michel, Bertrand Thirion, Olivier Grisel, Mathieu Blondel, Peter Prettenhofer, Ron Weiss, Vincent Dubourg, Jake Vanderplas, Alexandre Passos, David Cournapeau, Matthieu Brucher, Matthieu Perrot, and Édouard Duchesnay. 2011. Scikit-learn: Machine Learning in Python. *Journal of Machine Learning Research*. 12:2825-2830

Ted Underwood and Jordan Sellers. 2012. The Emergence of Literary Diction. *The Journal of Digital Humanities*, 1(2). http://journalofdigitalhumanities.org/1-2/the-emergence-of-literary-diction-by-ted-underwood-and-jordan-sellers/

Michelle Yeh. 1991. *Modern Chinese Poetry: Theory and Practice since 1917*. Yale University Press, New Haven, CT.

Linguistic Resources & Topic Models for the Analysis of Persian Poems

Ehsaneddin Asgari and Jean-Cédric Chappelier
Ecole Polytechnique Fédérale de Lausanne (EPFL)
School of Computer and Communication Sciences (IC)
CH-1015 Lausanne ; Switzerland
ehsaneddin.asgari@epfl.ch and jean-cedric.chappelier@epfl.ch

Abstract

This paper describes the usage of Natural Language Processing tools, mostly probabilistic topic modeling, to study semantics (word correlations) in a collection of Persian poems consisting of roughly 18k poems from 30 different poets. For this study, we put a lot of effort in the preprocessing and the development of a large scope lexicon supporting both modern and ancient Persian. In the analysis step, we obtained very interesting and meaningful results regarding the correlation between poets and topics, their evolution through time, as well as the correlation between the topics and the metre used in the poems. This work should thus provide valuable results to literature researchers, especially for those working on stylistics or comparative literature.

1 Context and Objectives

The purpose of this work is to use Natural Language Processing (NLP) tools, among which probabilistic topic models (Buntine, 2002; Blei et al., 2003; Blei, 2012), to study word correlations in a special type of Persian poems called "Ghazal" (غزل), one of the most popular Persian poem forms originating in 6th Arabic century.

Ghazal is a poetic form consisting of rhythmic couplets with a rhyming refrain (see Figure 1). Each couplet consists of two phrases, called hemistichs. Syllables in all of the hemistichs of a given Ghazal follow the same pattern of heavy and light syllables. Such a pattern introduces a musical rhythm, called *metre*. Metre is one of the most important properties of Persian poems and the reason why usual Persian grammar rules can be violated in poems, especially the order of the parts of speech. There exist about 300 metres in Persian poems, 270 of which are rare, the vast majority of poems composed only from 30 metres (Mojiry and Minaei-Bidgoli, 2008).

Figure 1: Elements of a typical Ghazal (by Hafez, calligraphed by K. Khoroush). Note that Persian is right to left in writing.

Ghazal traditionally deals with just one subject, each couplet focusing on one idea. The words in a couplet are thus very correlated. However, depending on the rest of the couplets, the message of a couplet could often be interpreted differently due to the many literature techniques that can be found in Ghazals, e.g. metaphors, homonyms, personification, paradox, alliteration.

For this study, we downloaded from the Ganjoor poems website[1], with free permission to use, a Ghazal collection corresponding to 30 poets, from Hakim Sanai (1080) to Rahi Moayyeri (1968), with a total of 17,939 Ghazals containing about 170,000 couplets. The metres, as determined by experts (Shamisa, 2004), are also provided for most poems.

[1] http://ganjoor.net/.

We put a lot of effort into the preprocessing, so as to provide more informative input to the modeling step. For this, we built a lexicon supporting both modern and ancient Persian, as explained in Section 2. In addition, we developed several preprocessing tools for Persian and adapted them to poems, as detailed in Section 3. In the analysis step, exploiting Probabilistic Topic Models (Blei, 2012), promising results were obtained as described in Section 4: strong correlation between poets and topics was found by the model, as well as relevant patterns in the dynamics of the topics over years; good correlation between topics and poem metre was also observed.

2 Modern and Ancient Persian Lexicon

This section presents the Persian lexicon we built, which supports both modern and ancient Persian words and morphology and provides lemmas for all forms. This lexicon could thus be useful to many research projects related to both traditional and modern Persian text processing. Its total size is about 1.8 million terms, including the online version[2] of the largest Persian Dictionary today (Dehkhoda, 1963). This is quite large in comparison with e.g. the morphological lexicon provided by Sagot & Walther (2010), of about $600k$ terms in total.

2.1 Verbs

Taking advantage of the verb root collection provided by Dadegan group (Rasooli et al., 2011), we conjugated all of the regular forms of the Persian verbs which exist in modern Persian using grammars provided by M. R. Bateni (1970), and added them with their root forms (lemmas) to the lexicon. We also added ancient grammatical forms, referring to ancient grammar books for Persian (Bateni, 1970; P. N. Xanlāri, 2009).

Persian verb conjugation seems to be simple: normally each verb has two roots, past and present. In each conjugated form, the corresponding root comes with some prefixes and attached pronouns in a predefined order. However, phonological rules introduce some difficulties through so-called *mediators*. For instance, the verb آراستن (**ârâstan**, meaning "*to decorate*" or "*to attire*") has آرا (**ârâ**) as present root and آراست (**ârâst**) as past root. Its injunctive form requires it to be preceded by بِ (**be**), leading to بارا (**beârâ**). However, according to phonological rules, when a consonant attaches to آ (**â**), a یـ (**y**) is introduced as a mediator. So the correct injunctive form is بیارا (**byârâ**, "*decorate!*").

Mediators occur mainly when a consonant comes before **â** or when a syllable comes after **â** or و (**u**). But the problem is slightly more complicated. For instance, the present verb for جستن (**jostan**, "*seeking*") is جو (**ju**). Thus when the pronoun ـَم (**am**, "*I*") is attached, the conjugated form should be جویم (**juyam**, "*I seek*"), with a mediator. However, the root **ju** has also a homograph **jav** (also written جو) which is the present root of جویدن (**javidan**, "*chewing*"). Since here و is pronounced **v**, not **u**, there is no need for a mediator and the final form is جوم (**javam**, "*I chew*"). Therefore, naively applying the above mentioned simple rules is wrong and we must proceed more specifically. To overcome this kind of problem, we studied the related verbs one by one and introduced the necessary exceptions.

In poems, things are becoming even more complicated. Since metre and rhyme are really key parts of the poem, poets sometimes waives the regular structures and rules in order to save the rhyme or the metre (Tabib, 2005). For instance, F. Araqi in one of his Ghazals decided to use the verb form می‌نایی (**mi-nâyi**, "*you are not coming*") which does not follow the mediator rules, as it must be می‌نیایی (**mi-naâyayi**). The poet decided to use the above form, which still makes sense, to preserve the metre.

The problem of mediators aside, the orders of parts in the verb structures are also sometimes changed to preserve the metre/rhyme. For instance in the future tense, the compound part of compound verbs has normally to come first. A concrete example is given by the verb جان خواهد سپرد (**jân xâhad sepord** means "*(s)he will give up his spirit and will die*"), which is written by Hafez as: خواهد سپرد جان (**xâhad sepord jân**). To tackle these variations, we included in our lexicon all the alternative forms mentioned by Tabib (2005).

As already mentioned, the considered poem collection ranges from 1080 to 1968. From a linguistics point of view some grammatical structures of the language have changed over this long period of time. For instance, in ancient Persian the prefix for

[2] http://www.loghatnaameh.org/.

the continuity of verb was همی (**hami**); today only می (**mi**) is used. Many kinds of changes could be observed when ancient grammars are compared to the modern one. The relevant structures to the mentioned period of time were extracted from a grammar book of ancient Persian (P. N. Xanlāri, 2009) and included in our lexicon.

Starting from the 4,162 infinitives provided by Dadegan group (Rasooli et al., 2011) and considering ancient grammars, mediators, and properties of poetic forms, we ended up with about 1.6 million different conjugated verb forms. The underlying new structures have exhaustively been tested by a native Persian graduate student in literature and linguistics. This validation took about one hundred hours of work, spot-checking all the conjugations for random selected infinitives.

2.2 Other words (than verbs)

The verbs aside, we also needed a complete list of other words. The existing usual Persian electronic lexica were insufficient for our purpose because they are mainly based on newspapers and do not necessarily support ancient words. For our purpose, the ongoing effort of Dehkhoda Online Dictionary[3] looked promising. Dehkhoda dictionnary (Dehkhoda, 1963) is the largest comprehensive Persian dictionary ever published, comprising 16 volumes (more than 27,000 pages), entailing over 45 years of efforts by Aliakbar Dehkhoda and other experts and it is still ongoing. The Dehkhoda Online Dictionary Council fortunately approved our request to use their work which currently contains 343,466 entries (for 234,425 distinct forms).

Besides the Dehkhoda Online Dictionary, we added the free Virastyar Persian lexicon[4]. Although the is size is one tenth of Dehkhoda's, it contains several new imported words, not found in Dehkhoda. All together, we ended up with a lexicon of 246,850 distinct surface forms. For each surface form, we also provide the list of corresponding roots (lemmas).

[3] `http://www.loghatnaameh.org/`.

[4] `http://www.virastyar.ir/data/`.

3 Preprocessing

Preprocessing is an essential part in NLP which usually plays an important role in the overall performance of the system. In this work, preprocessing for Persian Ghazals consists of tokenization, normalization, stemming/lemmatization and filtering.

3.1 Tokenization

The purpose of tokenization is to split the poems into word/token sequences. As an illustration, a hemistich like

شاه شمشاد قدان خسرو شیرین دهنان

is split into the following tokens:

شاه / شمشاد / قدان / خسرو / شیرین / دهنان.

The tokenization was done using separator characters like white spaces, punctuation, etc. However, half-spaces made this process quite complicated, as most of them appeared to be ambiguous.

Half-space is a hidden character which avoids preceding letters to be attached to the following letters; the letters in Persian having different glyphs when attached to the preceding letters or not.

For instance, می‌رفت (**mi-raft**, "*was going*"), here written with a half-space separating its two parts, **mi** (می) and **raft** (رفت) would be written میرفت without the half-space (notice the difference in the middle).

Half-spaces carry useful information, e.g. for recognizing compound words. However, they were not reliable enough in the poem collection used.

The main challenges we had to face related to half-spaces were related to continuous verbs. In Persian, continuous verbs have a prefix **mi** (می) which should be separated from the rest of the verb by a half-space. However, it was sometimes written using full-spaces and sometimes even without any space at all. For instance **mi-goft** ("*was saying*") should be written with a half-space: می‌گفت but was sometimes written using a full space: می گفت, and even sometimes without any separator: میگفت. The problem of identifying continuous verbs is even more complicated in poems because the prefix (**mi**) is the homograph of a word meaning "*wine*" (**mey:** می), quite frequent in Persian poems.

For dealing with continuous verbs, we apply the following heuristic: in the structure of continuous verbs, the prefix **mi** comes before the root of verbs, thus, if a root of a verb comes just after a **mi**, then we can consider it as a continuous verb. However, many **mi**'s meaning *wine* would be considered as prefixes using this too simple heuristic, because the most frequent letter in Persian آ (**â**) is also a verb root. For instance, in phrase **mey-e-âsemâni:** می آسمانی , **mey** means "*wine*" and the second part آسمانی means "*related to heaven*" (as an adjective, not a verb). To consider **mi** as a prefix, we thus constrained the token after it to start with a root longer than 2 letters.

The mentioned rule improves the process of tokenization. However, there are still some cases which are really complicated even for a human to decide. For instance, **mi-âlud:** می آلود ("*was polluting*") and **mey-âlud:** می آلود ("*polluted with wine*") are homographs in Persian; whose precise tokenization requires contextual information or even metre to decide which one is more suited. As a simple solution we can consider **mey-âlud** and any other known compound forms of **mey** as compound words and add them to our lexicon. Taking the advantages of this solution for such ambiguous words, we can identify if there is any ambiguity and given that there is some, we can pass all of them to the next processing steps, not deciding too soon.

Continuous verbs aside, present perfect verbs, prefix verbs, and compound verbs have also two parts which might be separated with half-space or full white-space. For instance, **rafteh-am** ("*have gone*") might appear with a half-space: رفته‌ام , without any separator: رفتهام , or with a full space: رفته ام.

Since the tokenization was complicated and requires linguistic knowledge, especially to properly handle half-spaces, we designed it in two steps: first a basic version to bootstrap the process before character normalization (next subsection), and later a refinement of the basic tokenization, taking advantage of the rich Persian lexicon we built.

As a first tokenization step, we took the advantage of the fact that the number of tokens in a hemistich is intuitively between four and ten, because of Ghazals' metre rules. We thus decided that when full-space tokenization had less than four tokens, then both full- and half-spaces must be considered as separators. If the number of tokens obtained this way is more than four, the tokenization is forwarded to the next step. Otherwise, if there is still less than four tokens, the hemistich is marked for manual checking. The number of hemistichs that required manual fixation was very low, about 40 out of 340,000.

3.2 Normalization

In Persian fonts, several letters have more than one form, because of different writing style related to different pronunciations; for instance **âmrika**: آمریکا, **emrika**: امریکا ("*America*"); and of different characters encoding of Arabic letters; for instance **anâr** ("*pomegranate*") might be written انار or أنار.

We get rid of these meaningless variations by normalizing the characters. This normalization has to come *after* basic tokenization because of the unreliable half-spaces, to be handled first, that interfere with the written form of some letters.

We first used *both* Arabic and Persian normalizers of Lucene[5]: in the Persian version, most of the cases are considered except different alefs (first letter of Persian alphabet), which are properly handled by the Arabic normalizer. We furthermore added the following rules to Lucene modules:

- Normalization for **vâv** and **ye**:

  There are two different forms of **vâv**: و or ؤ , which is rather Arabic, not preferred in Persian. For instance, word **mo'men** ("*believer*") could be written مومن or مؤمن.

  We have a similar case with **ye** which might be written ئـ or یـ. For instance, **âyine** ("*mirror*") might be written آیینه or آئینه.

- Some characters exist which are optional in Persian writing for instance light vowels, **tašdid** (sign of emphasis: ـّ in محمّد), and **tanvins**, three signs could be attached at the end of some words, e.g. ـً in حضوراً . Some of them were implemented in Lucene Arabic normalizer, some in the Persian normalizer and some in none of them.

- Removal of the optional **hamze** sign ء at the end of word, for instance: املاء.

- Removal (without any change in the meaning) of some Arabic characters that do not normally appear in Persian but were present in the corpus, e.g. ٍ (**tanvin kasre**), ٌ (**tanvin zamme**).

[5] `http://lucene.apache.org/`.

- Removal (without any change in the meaning) of adornment (calligraphy) characters, e.g. dashes, ْ (**sokun**), and ~ (**mad**).

As explained in the former subsection, the final tokenization was postponed due to the difficult ambiguities introduced by half-/full-space confusions. To finalized it after character normalization, taking the advantage of our lexicon, we considered all bigrams, trigrams and 4-grams of tokens obtained and checked whether they correspond to a valid form in the lexicon. Out of 2,876,929 tokens, we had 330,644 (valid) bigrams, 12,973 trigrams and 386 4-grams.

3.3 Stemming/Lemmatization

The purpose of stemming/lemmatization[6] is to regroup (using the same writing) words of similar root, in order to reduce (hopefully the non-significant part of) the variability of the documents processed.

Although a free Persian stemmer PerStem exists (Jadidinejad et al., 2009)[7], its limitations we observed (see below) encouraged us to build our own stemmer.

Since Persian is an affixive language, lemmatization is achieved by removing plural signs, attached pronouns, prefixes and suffixes to obtain the root. We thus collected a list of these and enriched it using affixes provided by Adib Tousi (1974) and by Tabtabai (2007). Then we designed a flowchart to iteratively remove the unwanted parts from the normalized token until we get a simple word contained in the lexicon or a word with a length of less than 4 letters. The experiences showed us it is more appropriate to remove prefixes first, then suffixes. Even in suffix removal, the removal order is a crucial issue. Since some words have more than one suffix and the set of suffixes is not a prefix-free set, a wrong removal order can leads to removing a wrong suffix and might result in finishing the removal too early, where there still exist some letters to be removed. For instance, the word کتابهایشان (**ketâbhâyešân**, "*their books*") should be reduced to کتاب (**ketâb**, "*book*"). It has three suffixes ها (**hâ**, plural marker), ی (**ye**, mediator) and شان (**šan**, "*their*" as a attached pronoun). However, **šan** has two prefixes which are also suffixes: ن (**N**, infinitive mark) and ان (**ân**, plural mark for nouns). Such cases are not considered in PerStem, and the affixes removal is stopped too early. In order to overcome this problem in our stemmer, we generated all of the possible combinations of affixes and add them to our affixes collection. Then the largest possible one is removed from the token at each step.

We then checked for the term in the lexicon and return its lemmas when matched. If we could not find any matched term in the lexicon, we manually check the token. Doing so, we realized that because of the missing/wrong spaces, most of these tokens wrongly attached to conjunctions. For this specific purpose, we partially modified the list of affixes and applied the stemmer again on these out of vocabulary forms, ending up with the proper information.

In the case of homographs, for instance نشستی that could be read as **nešasti** ("*you sat*") or as **našosti** ("*you did not wash*"), we pass *all* possible interpretations to the next processing step. For instance, the result of the lemmatization of نشستی is "'to sit' or 'to wash'", i.e. both lemmas.

3.4 Filtering

In order to reduce even further the input variability, some filtering has been performed based both on frequencies and on a standard list of "stop-words", some extremely common words which are normally meaningless (at least independently).

The general strategy for determining stop-words is to sort the terms by their frequencies in the collection, consider the most frequent ones and then filter them manually with respect to the domain. Doing so, we found stop-words well suited for the poem collection considered, which is slightly different from stop-words in normal Persian text (poem specific, and typographical error occurred in the corpus used). We also combined this set with a (manually chosen) subset of stop-words provided by K. Taghva (2003).

4 Topic Modeling

After preprocessing, we studied the correlations among words in Ghazals using "probabilistic topic

[6]Stemming reduces words to their stems, using rather crude algorithms and basic morphological rules, while lemmatization uses more advanced morphological analysis and lexical resources to find the root form, named lemma.

[7]http://www.ling.ohio-state.edu/~jonsafari/persian_nlp.html.

Figure 2: Probabilistic distribution over the topics (learned in an unsupervised manner) for one specific couplet: the horizontal axis stands for the topics and the vertical axis for the probability of each topic for the couplet considered. Notice how only a few topics are used in the couplet. The most probable words for the five most probable topics for this couplet are also provided on the right. On top, an example of a possible assignment of these topics to the words in the couplet considered is provided. Each color represents one of the 5 most probable topics.

models" (Buntine, 2002; Blei, 2012), more precisely Latent Dirichlet Allocation (LDA) (Blei et al., 2003)[8]. We looked into correlation between topics and poets, as well as between topics and metres, and obtained very interesting results.

4.1 Model

Probabilistic topic models are unsupervised generative models which represent documents as mixtures of *topics*, rather than (only) collections of terms (Blei, 2012). "Topics" are nothing else but probability distributions over the vocabulary that are learned in an unsupervised manner. Probabilistic topic models allow us to represent documents at a higher level (topics rather than words) with much fewer parameters. A typical example is given in Figure 2.

Taking advantage from conditional co-occurrences through topics, these models are able to take both polysemy and synonymy into account. To illustrate how such models behave, we could for instance consider the polysemic term

[8]We used Mallet software, version 2.0.7; `http://mallet.cs.umass.edu/`.

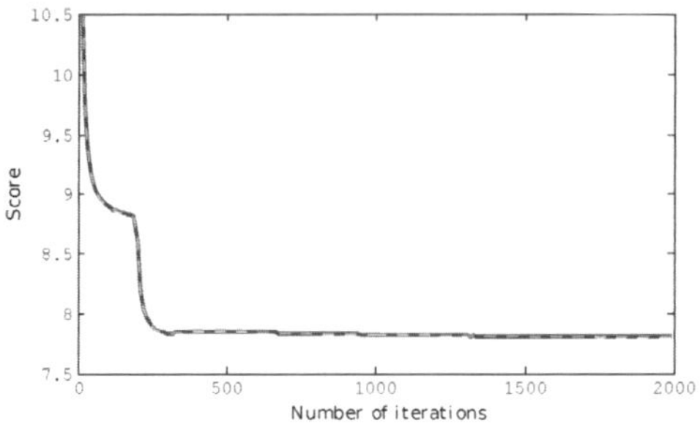

Figure 3: Learning score w.r.t number of iterations. After the iteration 200, hyper-parameter optimization starts and around 600 the score has converged. $\pm$1-standard-deviation curves determined using 1x10-fold cross validation cannot be distinguished from the average curve.

شیرین (**širin/Shirin**, meaning "*sweet*" but also standing for the name of a well-known woman from a famous story), which appeared in the ten most frequent terms of topics 413 and 337 (blue words in Table 1). Two topics presented in Table 1 are showing different contexts that can include **širin** as a keyword. Topic 413 appeared to refer to contexts related to sweetness, whereas topic 337 appeared to refer to a famous Persian tragic romance, "*Khosrow and Shirin*", a.k.a. "*Shirin and Farhad*".

Furthermore, since ambiguity (homonymy) is a literature technique, sometimes poets use **širin** somewhere that can refer to both contexts. That could be the reason why شکر (**šekar**, "*sugar*"), represented in green, appears in frequent terms of both topics.

One key issue using these kind of models regards the choice of the number of topics. To decide the appropriate number, we measured the model quality with held-out log-likelihood (estimated on validation set) using 1x10-fold cross validation (Wallach et al., 2009; Buntine, 2009).[9] We ran each fold for 2000 iterations (convergence checked; see Figure 3) doing hyper-parameter optimization (Wallach et al., 2010) after 200 iterations. We observe that the log-likelihood decreases, and stabilizes around 400/500 topics (see Figure 4). We thus considered 500 topics to be a good order of magnitude for this corpus.

[9]Note that the evaluation method implemented in Mallet is the biased method provided by Wallach (2009) and not the proper methods suggested by Buntine (2009).

Table 1: 10 Most probable terms chosen from three topics (among 500 topics).

Topic 290	Topic 413	Topic 337
candle =شمع	sugar =شکر	Shirin =شیرین
butterfly =پروانه	sweet =شیرین	Farhad =فرهاد
light =چراغ	poison =زهر	Khosrow =خسرو
to tear =درید،در	bitter =تلخ	mountain =کوه
to burn =سوخت،سوز	sour =ترش	to carve or to do =کندن or کردن
bright =روشن	sugar =قند	sweet life =شیرین جان
society =انجمن	mouth =دهان	mount cutting =کن کوه
clique =محفل	honey =شهد	axe =تیشه
fire =اتش	palate =کام	blessed =خوبان
flame =شعله	bitterness =تلخی	sugar =شکر

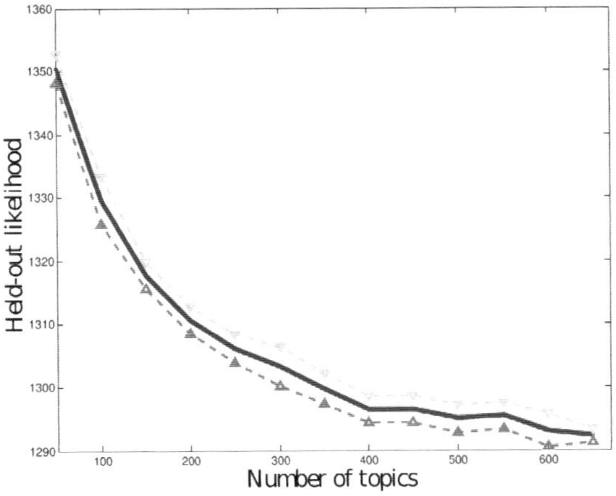

Figure 4: Held-out log-likelihood versus number of topics. ±1-stand.-dev. curves obtained by 1x10-fold cross-validation are also shown (dashed lines).

Figure 5: Correlation between (automatically found) topics and poets: the joint probability $P(\text{topic, poet})$ is plotted in dark shades; the darker the shade, the higher the probability. The dark mark along the diagonal thus illustrates a very good correlation (conditional probability, in fact) between topics and poets. For a better visualization, both rows and columns have here been reordered.

4.2 Correlation between Topics and Poets

Good correlation between some topics and poets has been observed. To investigate this correlation further, the joined probability of topics and poets is measured and the results are shown in Figure 5. It can be observed that there is a strong correlation between poets and topics. Some general topics (used by all the poets) also appear (as vertical darker lines).

Another good illustration of this correlation is given in Figure 6 which illustrates the proportions of four different topics for the 30 poets ordered by their lifetime. Some relevant patterns can be observed. For instance, the topic related to "Joseph" (blue) and the one related to "Mirror" (violet) are correlated. In Persian literature, Joseph is the symbol of beauty and

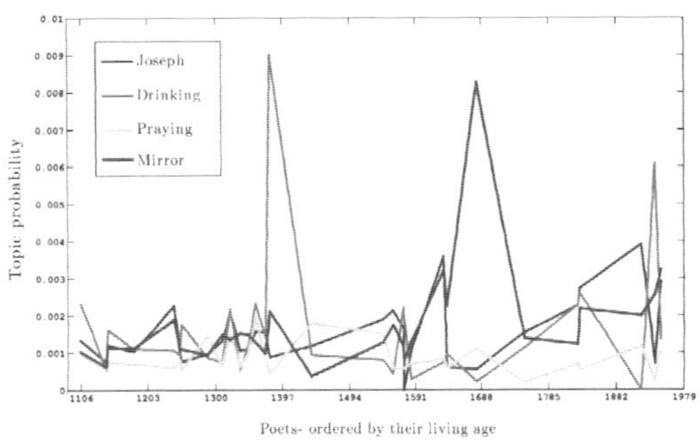

Figure 6: The probability of four different (automatically found) topics over the time. X-axis shows the middle of lifetime of the poets.

beauty can be perceived by means of the mirror. This is the reason why these two topics are somehow correlated. Moreover, the "Mirror" topic has an independent peak around 1700 A.D. This corresponds to Bidel Dehlave, so-called "poet of mirrors" (Kadkani, 2007), who very often refers to mirrors in his poems.

Another pattern relates to drinking, which in Persian mystical literature refers to a grace from heaven. The main era of mystical literature is between 1300 and 1400 AD. As it can be observed from Figure 6, "Praying" and "Drinking" topics have similar curves in this time period, as expected. The independent peak corresponds to the poet Awhadi Maraghai who uses words related to drinking very much.

4.3 Correlation between Topics and Metre

There is supposed to be a relation between the happiness or sadness of the words in a poem and its melody (metre). Vahidian Kamyar (Kamyar, 1985), for instance, provides a list of metres and their corresponded feeling.

We thus also wanted to investigated whether there was any correlation between the metres and the topics learned in an unsupervised manner. To answer this question, we encoded the 30 metres provided in the original corpus as a (new random) term each, and then added the corresponding "metre term" once to each couplet. Then a topic model has been estimated.

The results obtained confirmed Kamyar's observations. For instance, the topics that have as probable term the "metre term" corresponding to the metre Kamyar associates to requiem, parting, pain, regret and complain (فعلن فعلاتن فعلاتن فعلاتن) are presented in Table 2. As you can see all of the three topics presented are showing a kind of sadness.

Table 2: 8 Most probable terms chosen from three topics related to a metre usually related to sadness.

Topic 43 (≃ "Suffering")	
رنجید،رنج =to suffer	راحت =comfort
رنج =pain	شفا =healing
بیمار =patient	رنجور =ill
طبیب =doctor	بیماری =illness
Topic 154 (≃ "Crying")	
اشك =tear	سیل =flood
چکید،چك =to trickle	روان =fluid
مژه =eyelash	اشکم =my tear
گریه =cry	سرشك =drop
Topic 279 (≃ "Love and Burn")	
سوخت،سوز =to burn	شمع =candle
سوخته =burned (adj.)	عشق =love
اتش =fire	عود =oud (≃ guitar)
سوخت =burned or fuel (N.)	جگر =liver (≃ heart)

"Love & Burn" topic is not surprising for people used to Persian poetry as the butterfly—candle metaphor is often used. reminding of a common belief among Persians that butterflies love candles to the ultimate level of love so as to vanish in the presence of candle by burning in its fire.

5 Conclusion

With this study, we show that we can fruitfully analyze Persian poems, both for modern and ancient Persian, using NLP tools. This was not a priori obvious due to their specific nature (special form, ancient vocabulary and grammar, ...).

We put a lot of effort into the preprocessing, adapting it to poems, and in the development of a large scope lexicon supporting both modern and ancient Persian. In the analysis step, exploiting the power of probabilistic topic models, we obtained very interesting and meaningful results. We found strong correlation between poets and topics, as well as relevant patterns in the dynamics of topics over years. Correlation between the topics present in the poems and their metre was also observed.

As far as we know, this study is the first semantic study of Persian poems from a computational point of view. It provides valuable results for literature researchers, specially for those working in stylistics.

Follow-up work will include building a semantic search tool and a poem recommender system.

Acknowledgments The authors would like to warmly thank Mrs. Fereshteh Jafari for her help with the validation of the verb lexicon as well as the anonymous reviewers for their helpful comments.

References

[Bateni1970] M. R. Bateni. 1970. *The description of grammar structure in Persian language (توصیف ساختمان دستوری زبان فارسی)*. AmirKabir, Tehran.

[Blei et al.2003] D. M. Blei, A. Y. Ng, and M. I. Jordan. 2003. Latent Dirichlet allocation. *Journal of Machine Learning Research*, 3:993–1022, January.

[Blei2012] D. M. Blei. 2012. Probabilitic topic models. *Communications of the ACM*, 55(4):77–84, April.

[Buntine2002] W. Buntine. 2002. Variational extensions to EM and multinomial PCA. In *Proc. of ECML'02*, volume 2430 of *LNAI*, pages 23–34.

[Buntine2009] W. Buntine. 2009. Estimating likelihoods for topic models. In *Proc. of ACML'09*, volume 5828 of *LNAI*, pages 51–64.

[Dehkhoda1963] A.-A. Dehkhoda, editor. 1963. *The Dehkhoda Dictionary*. Tehran University Press.

[Jadidinejad et al.2009] A. H. Jadidinejad, F. Mahmoudi, and J. Dehdari. 2009. Evaluation of PerStem: a simple and efficient stemming algorithm for persian. In *Proc. 10th Cross-Language Evaluation Forum Conf. (CLEF'09)*, pages 98–101. Springer-Verlag.

[Kadkani2007] M. R. Shafiee Kadkani. 2007. *Poet of mirrors (شاعر آیینه‌ها)*. Agaah.

[Kamyar1985] T. Vahidan Kamyar. 1985. Metre in persian poems (اوزان ایقاعی شعر فارسی). Technical report, Department of Literature and Human Sciences, Ferdowsi University of Mashhad.

[Mojiry and Minaei-Bidgoli2008] M. M. Mojiry and B. Minaei-Bidgoli. 2008. Persian poem rhythm recognition: A new application of text mining. In *Proc. of IDMC'08*, Amir Kabir University.

[P. N. Xanlāri2009] E. Mostasharniya P. N. Xanlāri. 2009. *The Historical Grammar of Persian Language (دستور تاریخی زبان فارسی)*. Tose'eye Iran, 7th edition. (1st edititon: 1995).

[Rasooli et al.2011] M. S. Rasooli, A. Moloodi, M. Kouhestani, and B. MinaeiBidgoli. 2011. A syntactic valency lexicon for persian verbs: The first steps towards persian dependency treebank. In 5th *Language & Technology Conference (LTC): Human Language Technologies: a Challenger for Computer Science and Linguistics*.

[Sagot and Walther2010] B. Sagot and G. Walther. 2010. A morphological lexicon for the persian language. In *Proc. of the 7th Conf. on Int. Language Resources and Evaluation (LREC'10)*, pages 300–303.

[Shamisa2004] S. Shamisa. 2004. *An introduction to prosody (آشنایی با قافیه و عروض)*. Mitra, 4th edition.

[Tabatabai2007] A. Tabatabai. 2007. Persian language etymology (صرف زبان فارسی). *Bokhara Magazine*, 63:212–242, November.

[Tabib2005] S. M. T. Tabib. 2005. Some of grammatical structures are used in persian poems (برخی ساختارهای دستوری گونه‌ی شعری). *Persian Academy (Farhangestan)*, 1:65–78, February.

[Taghva et al.2003] K. Taghva, R. Beckley, and M. Sadeh. 2003. A list of farsi stopwords. Technical Report 2003–01, ISRI.

[Tousi1974] M. A. Adib Tousi. 1974. The affixes in persian language (وندهای فارسی). *Gohar*, 17:432–436, July.

[Wallach et al.2009] H. M. Wallach, I. Murray, R. Salakhutdinov, and D. Mimno. 2009. Evaluation methods for topic models. In *Proc. 26th An. Int. Conf. on Machine Learning (ICML'09)*, pages 1105–1112. ACM.

[Wallach et al.2010] H. Wallach, D. Mimno, and A. McCallum. 2010. Rethinking LDA: Why priors matter. In Y. Bengio, D. Schuurmans, J. Lafferty, C. K. I. Williams, and A. Culotta, editors, *Advances in Neural Information Processing Systems 22 (NIPS'09)*, pages 1973–1981.

The desirability of a corpus of online book responses

Peter Boot
Huygens ING
PO Box 90754
2509 HT The Hague
The Netherlands
peter.boot@huygens.knaw.nl

Abstract

This position paper argues the need for a comprehensive corpus of online book responses. Responses to books (in traditional reviews, book blogs, on booksellers' sites, etc.) are important for understanding how readers understand literature and how literary works become popular. A sufficiently large, varied and representative corpus of online responses to books will facilitate research into these processes. This corpus should include context information about the responses and should remain open to additional material. Based on a pilot study for the creation of a corpus of Dutch online book response, the paper shows how linguistic tools can find differences in word usage between responses from various sites. They can also reveal response type by clustering responses based on usage of either words or their POS-tags, and can show the sentiments expressed in the responses. LSA-based similarity between book fragments and response may be able to reveal the book fragments that most affected readers. The paper argues that a corpus of book responses can be an important instrument for research into reading behavior, reader response, book reviewing and literary appreciation.

1 Introduction

The literary system does not consist of authors and works alone. It includes readers (or listeners) and their responses to literary works. Research into reception is an important subfield of literary studies (e.g. Goldstein and Machor, 2008). Shared attention to stories may have evolved as way of learning to understand others and to increase bonding (Boyd, 2009). Discussing literature may thus be something that we are wired to do, and that we do indeed wherever possible: today on Amazon, on weblogs, and on Twitter, and in earlier days in newspapers and letters. These responses to books are important both as documentation of the ways literary works are read and understood, and because they help determine works' short- and long-term success.

This position paper argues that what we need, therefore, is a large and representative corpus of book responses. 'Book response' in this paper includes any opinion that responds to a book, i.e. traditional book reviews, book-based discussion, opinions given on booksellers' sites, on Twitter, thoughtful blog posts, and the like. The word 'books' here is meant to refer to all genres, including literature as well as more popular genres such as fantasy, thrillers, comics, etc. Section 2 of the paper discusses the importance and research potential of book responses. Section 3 reviews related research. In section 4, I outline the properties that this corpus should have. Section 5 describes a Dutch pilot corpus and shows some aspects of this corpus that lend themselves to analysis with linguistic and stylometric tools. Section 6 presents conclusions and directions for future work.

The author of this paper is not a computational linguist, but has a background in literary studies and digital humanities. The intention is to create a dialogue between literary studies and computational linguistics about fruitful ways to investigate book responses, their relations to the books they respond to and their effects on short-term or long-term appreciation.

2 Book responses and their importance

Evaluating books and talking about our response is a very natural thing to do (Van Peer, 2008). In a professionalized form, the discipline of literary criticism has a long and distinguished tradition (Habib, 2005). But 'ordinary' readers too have always talked about their reading experiences (Long, 2003; Rehberg Sedo, 2003). The written output of these reflections and discussions has been an important source for reading and reception studies. Proof of this importance is e.g. the existence of the Reading Experience Database (RED) that collects experiences of reading as documented in letters, memoirs and other historic material (Crone et al., 2011). Halsey (2009) e.g. shows how this database can help study changes in stylistic preferences over time.

One reason for the importance of written book responses is that they provide documentation of how works affect their readers: they show what elements of the reading experience readers consider important enough to write down and share with friends and fellow-readers. To some extent at least this will be determined by the elements of the book that were most significant to the reader and that he or she is most likely to remember. Unlike in earlier historic periods, this sort of evidence today is plentiful and researchers should take advantage of this. Spontaneous written responses to reading are not the only way of assessing the effects of (literary) reading. Experimental research (Miall, 2006) and other approaches have an important place. Today's online book responses, however, are unique in that they are produced spontaneously by ordinary readers and have an ecological validity that other research data lack. (Which does, of course, not imply we should take everything that people write online at face value).

A second reason for the importance of written book responses is that their role as (co-)determiners, or at least predictors, of literary success is well-documented. In the wake of a large body of research on movie reviews (e.g. Liu, 2006), this was established for reviews on booksellers' sites by (Chevalier and Mayzlin, 2006). For traditional (newspaper) reviews, their effects on long-term success (canonization) have been shown in e.g. (Ekelund and Börjesson, 2002; Rosengren, 1987).

If reading responses are that important for the study of literature and its effects, it follows we need to understand them better. We need tools that can analyze their style, rhetorical structure, topics, and sentiment, and these tools should be sensitive to the many different sorts of readers, responses and response sites that form part of the landscape of online book discussion. We also need tools that can help us see relationships between the responses and the works that they respond to, in terms of topics and narrative (what characters and plot developments do reviewers respond to), as well as at higher (cognitive, emotional and moral) levels. An important step towards such tools is the creation of a representative corpus that can provide a test bed for tool development.

3 Related research

Online book discussion is a wide field that can be studied from many different angles. I discuss first a number of studies that do not use computational methods. Online book reviewing has often been discussed negatively in its relation to traditional reviews (McDonald, 2007; Pool, 2007). Certainly problematic aspects of online reviews are the possibilities of plagiarism and fraud (David and Pinch, 2006). Verboord (2010) uses a questionnaire to investigate the perceived legitimacy of internet critics. Online critics' role in canonization was investigated in (Grafton, 2010). That online reviews do have an influence on books sales was established by (Chevalier and Mayzlin, 2006), and specifically for books by women and popular fiction in (Verboord, 2011). Many librarians have looked at what online book discussion sites can mean for the position of the library, library cataloguing and book recommendations (Pera and Ng, 2011; Pirmann, 2012). Online book discussion as an extension of the reading group is discussed in e.g. (Fister, 2005). A look at the whole field, from a genre perspective, is given in (Boot, 2011). Steiner (2010) looks specifically at Swedish weblogs; (Steiner, 2008) discusses Amazon reviews, as does (Domsch, 2009). Gutjahr (2002) sent out a survey to posters of Amazon reviews. Finally, (Miller, 2011) investigates how book blogs can help develop the habits of mind required for literary reading.

Researchers that have used more or less sophisticated linguistic technology to investigate online book responses have done so with a number of different questions in mind. (Boot et al., 2012) sought to characterize responses from different site types based on word usage. Much effort has gone into the analysis of review sentiment, which has clear practical applications in marketing. (Taboada et al., 2011) use a lexicon-based approach; (Okanohara and Tsujii, 2005) a machine learning approach. (De Smedt and Daelemans, 2012a) create a Dutch sentiment lexicon based on reviews at an online bookseller. The helpfulness of online reviews has been investigated by e.g. (Tsur and Rappoport, 2009) while (Mukherjee and Liu, 2012) have modeled review comments. From an information retrieval perspective, the INEX social book search competition has explored the use of online reviews from Amazon and LibraryThing to create book recommendations (Koolen et al., 2012). A proposal for using text mining and discourse analysis techniques on pre-internet reviews is (Taboada et al., 2006). (Finn, 2011) used named entity recognition in reviews of a single writer in order to explore the 'ideational network' associated with her work.

It does not seem unfair to say that most of the computer-based linguistic research done into online book responses has been motivated by practical, if not commercial aims. Much of it was published in marketing journals. Computational linguistic research as a tool for understanding the variety of online book response is still at a very early stage of development.

4 A corpus of book responses

A corpus of book responses should present researchers with a varied, representative, and sufficiently large collection of book responses. It should not be a closed corpus but continue to grow. It should contain not just response texts but also include the metadata that describes and contextualizes the responses.

Varied: the responses should be taken from as wide a selection of sites as is possible. Sites are very different with regards to the active reviewers, their audience, the books that are discussed, the responses' function and the explicit and implicit expectations about what constitutes a proper response (Boot, 2011). Pragmatic aspects of the response (e.g. a response given on a weblog where the responder is the main author vs. a response in a forum where the responder is just one participant in a group discussion) obviously help determine both content and style of the response and tools that analyze responses should take account of these differences in setting.

Another respect in which variety is important is book genre. Much has been written about differences in book appreciation between e.g. readers of popular fiction and 'high' literature (Von Heydebrand and Winko, 1996). A response corpus should present researchers with a large body of responses from readers of a wide selection of genres (popular fiction, literature, non-fiction, essays, poetry, etc.), irrespective of its medium of publication (paper, e-book, online).

Representative: there is no need for this corpus to be strictly proportional with respect to site type or book genre. Still, it is important for all types and genres to be represented. Given the need to request permission from copyright holders, it will probably be impossible to achieve a truly representative corpus.

Sufficiently large: the required size of the corpus will depend on the sort of analysis that one tries to do. It is clear that analysis that goes beyond the collection level, e.g. at the book genre level, or at the level of individual reviewers, will need substantial amounts of text. A rule of thumb might be that collections should preferably contain more than a thousand responses and more than a million words.

Open: As new forms of computer-mediated communication continue to evolve, the ways of responding to and talking about books will also change. The corpus should facilitate research into these changes, and be regularly updated with collections from new site types.

Metadata: book response text acquires a large part of its meaning from its context. To facilitate research into many aspects of these responses it is important for the corpus to store information about that context. That information should include at least the site that the response was taken from, the response date, whatever can be known about the author of the response, and, if available, the book that the response responds to. Figure 1shows the relevant entities.

We will not discuss the data model in detail. Sites can contain multiple collections of responses, with different properties. Some sites for instance contain both commissioned reviews and user reviews. Weblogs contains posts by the blog owner and responses to those posts. Book theme sites often carry review sections and discussion forums. When analyzing a response, it is important to be aware what section the response belongs to. Book responses can also be written in response to other posts, be it in a discussion forum, on Twitter, or on a book-based social networking site. Book responses can be tagged, and the tags may carry valuable information about book topics, book appreciation or other book information. Responses are written by persons, sometimes unknown, who may own a site (as with blogs) or be among many people active on a site, or perhaps on multiple sites. Reviewers sometimes write profile texts about themselves that also discuss their book preferences. On some sites (book SNS's, Twitter) reviewers may strike up friendships or similar relationships. Some sites also allow people to list the books they own and/or their favorite books. Finally, meaningful use of book level data will often require being able to group multiple versions (manifestations) of the same work.

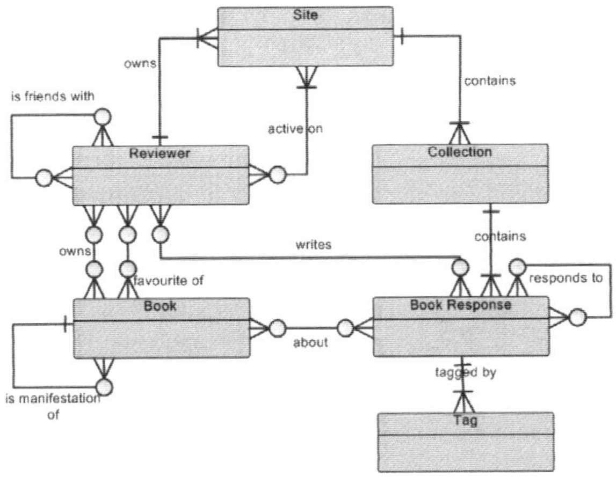

Figure 1. Book response corpus data model

For most collections, extracting the information carried by the respective entities mentioned is not a trivial task. Book shop review pages will probably contain an ISBN somewhere near the review, but forums probably will not and a tweet with an ISBN number is certainly unusual. And even if a response is ostensibly about book A, it may very well also discuss book B. Reviewer information will also be hard to obtain, as many reviews (e.g. on booksellers' sites) are unsigned.

5 Pilot study

For a pilot study that explores the research potential of online book response, I have been collecting Dutch-language book responses from a number of sites. The size of the pilot corpus and its subcollections is given in table 1. The pilot corpus contains responses from a number of weblogs, from online review magazine 8Weekly, book-based social network site watleesjij.nu ('whatareyoureading.now)', book publicity, reviews and user reviews from thriller site Crimezone, a collection of print reviews (from multiple papers and magazines) about Dutch novelist Arnon Grunberg, print reviews from Dutch newspaper NRC and publicity from the NRC web shop. The collection should be extended with responses from other site types (e.g. forums, twitter, bookseller reviews) other book genres (e.g. fantasy, romance, poetry) and perhaps other text genres (e.g. book news, interviews).

Collection	**Article genre**	**Response count**	**Word count (*1000)**
8weekly	review	2273	1512
weblogs	blog post	6952	3578
watleesjij.nu	user review	28037	2515
crimezone book desc	publicity	3698	462
crimezone review	review	3696	1622
crimezone userrev	user review	9163	1537
grunberg	print review	196	187
NRC web shop	publicity	1345	198
NRC reviews	print review	1226	1133
Total		**56586**	**12744**

Table 1. Present composition of pilot corpus of responses

I have done a number of experiments in order to explore the potential for computational linguistic analysis of book responses.

5.1 Measure response style and approach using LIWC

As a first test, I investigated word usage in the book responses using LIWC (Pennebaker et al., 2007; Zijlstra et al., 2004). Figure 2 shows the usage of first person pronouns on the respective site types. The pattern conforms to what one would expect: on the book SNS watleesjij.nu, where readers give personal opinions, 'I' predominates, as it does in the Crimezone user reviews, and to a lesser extent in the weblogs. In the commissioned reviews both in print (NRC newspaper and Grunberg collection) and online (8Weekly) 'we' prevails, as reviewers have to maintain an objective stance. Interestingly, the Crimezone book descriptions manage to avoid first person pronouns almost completely.

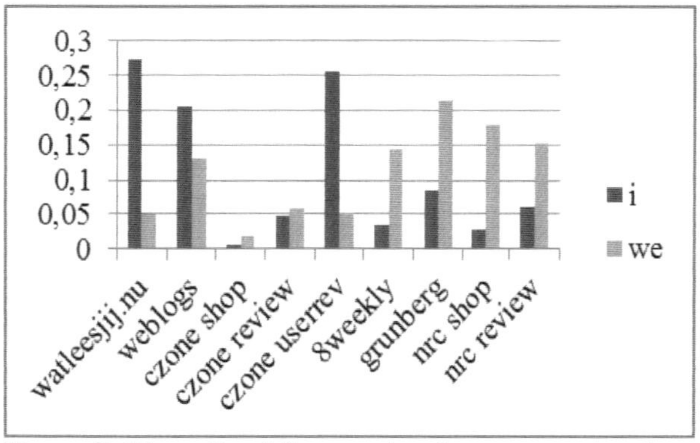

Figure 2. Normalized frequencies first person singular and first person plural pronouns

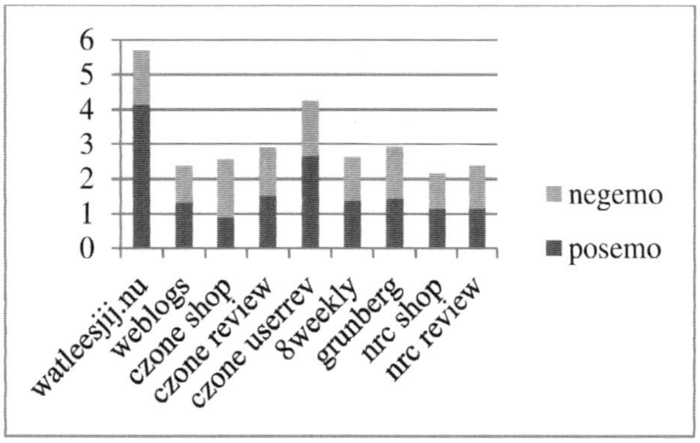

Figure 3. Positive and negative emotion word frequencies

A similar result appears when we chart positive and negative emotion words (Figure 3). Especially positive emotions are often expressed on watleesjij.nu and in the Crimezone user reviews. In this case the group of informal sites does not include the weblogs, perhaps because the weblogs included in the pilot corpus are blogs at the intellectual end of the spectrum. Also interesting is the high proportion of negative emotion in the Crimezone book descriptions, perhaps because in the case of thrillers emotions like fear and anxiety can function as recommendations.

From these examples it is clear that word usage on the respective sites shows meaningful variation that will profit from further research. Investigation into these patterns at the level of individual reviewers (e.g. bloggers) should begin to show individual styles of responding to literature.

5.2 Site stylistic similarities

As a second test, I looked into writing style, asking whether the styles on the respective sites are sufficiently recognizable to allow meaningful clustering. For each of the collections, except for the weblogs, I created five files of 20000 words each and used the tools for computational stylometry described in (Eder and Rybicki, 2011) to derive a clustering, based on the 300 most frequent words. Figure 4 shows the results.

It is interesting to note that all except the watleesjij.nu (book SNS) samples are stylistically consistent enough to be clustered by themselves. It is even more interesting to note that the book descriptions from the NRC (newspaper) shop cluster with the descriptions taken from the Crimezone site, that the reviews in online magazine 8Weekly cluster with the printed reviews, and that the Crimezone reviews, commissioned and user-contributed, cluster with the watleesjij.nu reviews. This may be related to the fact that there are a large number of thriller aficionados on watleesjij.nu, or to Crimezone reviews being significantly different from traditional reviews. Again, this seems a fruitful area for further investigation, only possible in the context of a large corpus containing different text types.

In order to exclude the possibility that this clustering is based on content words (e.g. words related to crime), I repeated the experiment using bi-grams of the words' POS-tags, as derived by the Pattern toolset (De Smedt and Daelemans, 2012b). The resulting figure, not reproduced here, is very similar to Figure 4. This result leads to another question: what sort of syntactic constructions are specific to which site types? And can we connect these stylistic differences to the approach to literature that these sites take?

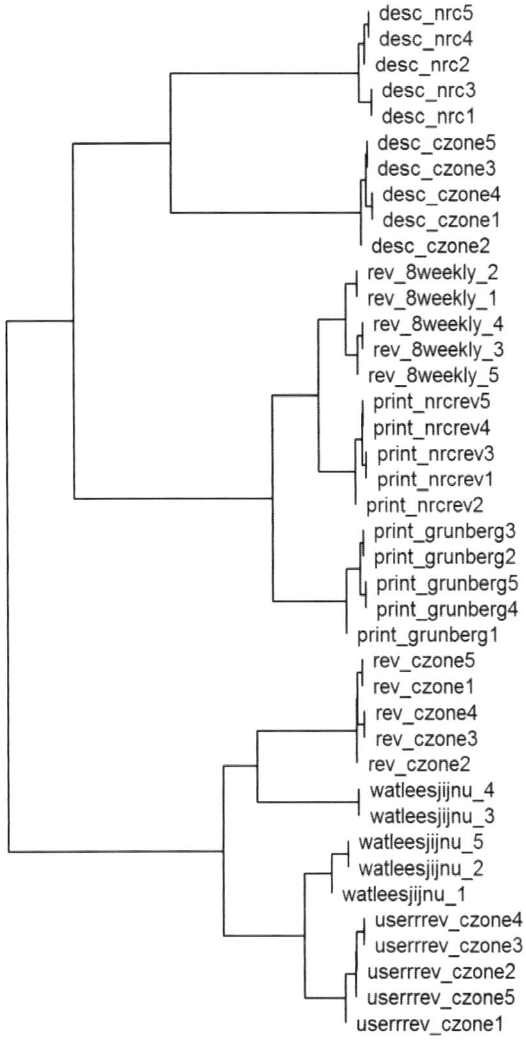

Figure 4. Clustering of 20000-word review texts based on 300 most frequent words.

5.3 Response sentiment analysis

In a third experiment, I applied the sentiment lexicon embedded in the Pattern toolset to the responses in those collections that include ratings. I predict a positive rating (i.e. above or equal to the collection median) when the sentiment as measured by Pattern is above 0.1, and compute precision, recall and F1-value for this prediction (see Figure 5). Results on the book SNS watleesjij.nu are similar to the results reported by (De Smedt and Daelemans, 2012a) for reviews from bookseller bol.com, perhaps because the responses on the two sites are similar. As expected, the results are considerably worse for the longer reviews on 8Weekly and NRC. That precision should be as high as .84 for the Crimezone reviews is somewhat of a mystery.

While it is not unexpected that the sentiment prediction quality should be higher for the sites with simpler reviews, this does imply a challenge for researchers of sentiment analysis. Without accurately gauging response sentiment (and many other response properties) measuring literary impact from responses will remain illusory.

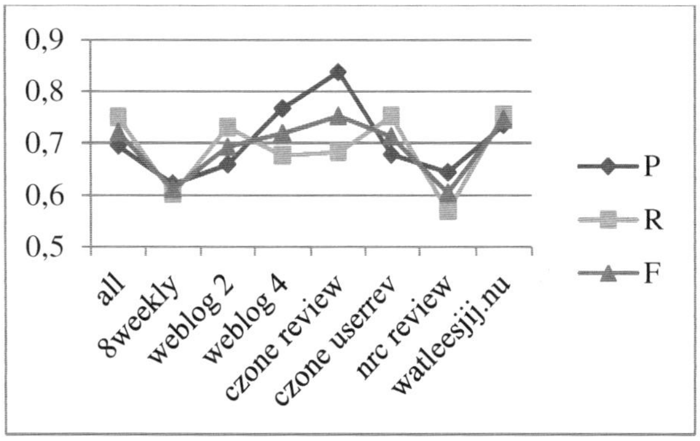

Figure 5. Prediction of positive or negative rating: precision, recall and F-score

5.4 Semantic similarities between book fragments and responses

A final experiment is based on the assumption that the semantics of book response texts to some extent reflect the semantics of the books they respond to. If that is true, it should be possible to determine the chapters that most impressed readers by comparing the book's and the reviews' semantic content. In order to test the assumption, I used Latent Semantic Analysis (LSA) (Landauer et al., 2007; Řehůřek and Sojka, 2010) to measure the distances between 400-word fragments taken from the novel *Tirza* by Dutch novelist Arnon Grunberg and 60 reviews of the book taken from book SNS watleesjij.nu. In order to compensate for potential similarities between book fragments and any reviews, rather than with reviews specifically of this book, I also measured semantic distances between the book's fragments and a set of random reviews from the same site, and subtracted those from the distances with the *Tirza* reviews. In order to test how these distances relate to the book's content, I computed LIWC scores for the fragments and then correlations between these LIWC scores and the LSA distances. For e.g. LIWC category 'family', a very important subject for this book, the correlation is positive and highly significant (.34, $p < .0001$).

Further experimentation with other books, other review collections and other LSA models is clearly needed. It is too early to say whether LSA indeed offers a viable approach for determining the book fragments most closely related to review texts, but this is clearly a promising result. Being able to connect measurable aspects of books with impact in reviews would help us understand how books affect their readers.

6 Conclusion

This paper adopts a broad conception of the object of literary studies, taking it to include the individual and social responses that literature elicits. I argued here that the (plentifully available) online book responses are important to literary studies, both as evidence (because they document the reception of literary works) and as objects (because they help determine works' short and long term popularity). If only because of the numbers of these responses, we need computational linguistic tools in order to analyze and understand them. Because the responses published on the various response platforms are in many respects very different, potential tools would need to be developed with these differences in mind. A good way to ensure this is to create an appropriately large and representative corpus of online book response. On the basis of a Dutch pilot corpus we saw that existing linguistic tools can reveal some of the differences between the respective platforms. They are currently unable, however, to perform any deeper analysis of these differences, let alone a deeper analysis of the relations between responses and books.

Naturally, written book response can only inform us about the reading experience of those that take the trouble of writing down and publishing their response. Even though those who provide book response are by no means a homogeneous group, it is clear that the proposed corpus would necessarily be selective, and should not be our only method of studying reader response. This is less of an issue when studying how books become popular and eventually canonized, as those who don't participate in the discussions will, for that very reason, be less influential.

With these caveats, there are a number of areas that a corpus of online book response would help investigate. Among these are:

- the responses themselves and their respective platforms: what language is used, what topics are discussed, what is their structure? What do they reveal about the literary norms that (groups of) readers apply?
- the relations between responses: we should be able to answer the questions about influence. What sort of discussions are going on about literature on which platforms? Which participants are most influential? Can response styles reveal these influences?
- what the responses show about the reading experience: we'd like to know how books (both books in general and specific books) affect people, what attracts people in books, what they remember from books, what they like about them, etc. What passages do they quote from the books they respond to? What characteristic words do they adopt?
- what the responses show about readers: as the corpus should facilitate selection by responder, we should be able to investigate the role of the reader in book response. Do responders' writing styles predict their ratings? Do people who like, say, James Joyce dislike science fiction? And can their book responses tell us why?

Many of these phenomena are interesting at multiple levels. They are interesting at the level of the individual reader, for whom reading in general and specific books are important. They are interesting at a sociological level, as discussions help determine books' popularity or even canonization. Finally, at the level of the book, study of book responses can show what readers, individually and in groups, take away from a book. In this respect especially, study of book responses is a necessary complement to study of the literary text.

References

Boot, Peter. 2011. Towards a Genre Analysis of Online Book Discussion: socializing, participation and publication in the Dutch booksphere. *Selected Papers of Internet Research* IR 12.0.

Boot, Peter, Van Erp, Marieke, Aroyo, Lora, and Schreiber, Guus. 2012. The changing face of the book review. Paper presented at *Web Science 2012*, Evanston (IL).

Boyd, Brian. 2009. *On the origin of stories: Evolution, cognition, and fiction*. Cambridge MA: Harvard University Press.

Chevalier, Judith A., and Mayzlin, Dina. 2006. The effect of word of mouth on sales: Online book reviews. *Journal of Marketing Research* 43:345-354.

Crone, Rosalind, Halsey, Katry, Hammond, Mary, and Towheed, Shafquat. 2011. The Reading Experience Database 1450-1945 (RED). In *The history of reading. A reader*, eds. Shafquat Towheed, Rosalind Crone and Katry Halsey, 427-436. Oxon: Routledge.

David, Shay, and Pinch, Trevor. 2006. Six degrees of reputation: The use and abuse of online review and recommendation systems. *First Monday* 11.

De Smedt, Tom, and Daelemans, Walter. 2012a. "Vreselijk mooi!" (terribly beautiful): A Subjectivity Lexicon for Dutch Adjectives. Paper presented at *Proceedings of the 8th Language Resources and Evaluation Conference (LREC'12)*.

De Smedt, Tom, and Daelemans, Walter. 2012b. Pattern for Python. *The Journal of Machine Learning Research* 13:2031-2035.

Domsch, Sebastian. 2009. Critical genres. Generic changes of literary criticism in computer-mediated communication. In *Genres in the Internet: issues in the theory of genre*, eds. Janet Giltrow and Dieter Stein, 221-238. Amsterdam: John Benjamins Publishing Company.

Eder, Maciej, and Rybicki, Jan. 2011. Stylometry with R. In *Digital Humanities 2011: Conference Abstracts*, 308-311. Stanford University, Stanford, CA.

Ekelund, B. G., and Börjesson, M. 2002. The shape of the literary career: An analysis of publishing trajectories. *Poetics* 30:341-364.

Finn, Edward F. 2011. The Social Lives of Books: Literary Networks in Contemporary American Fiction, Stanford University: PhD.

Fister, Barbara. 2005. Reading as a contact sport. *Reference & User Services Quarterly* 44:303-309.

Goldstein, Philip, and Machor, James L. 2008. *New directions in American reception study*. New York: Oxford University Press, USA.

Grafton, Kathryn. 2010. Paying attention to public readers of Canadian literature: popular genre systems, publics, and canons, University of British Columbia: PhD.

Gutjahr, Paul C. 2002. No Longer Left Behind: Amazon.com, Reader-Response, and the Changing Fortunes of the Christian Novel in America. *Book History* 5:209-236.

Habib, M. A. R. 2005. *A history of literary criticism: from Plato to the present*. Malden, MA: Blackwell.

Halsey, Katie. 2009. 'Folk stylistics' and the history of reading: a discussion of method. *Language and Literature* 18:231-246.

Koolen, Marijn, Kamps, Jaap, and Kazai, Gabriella. 2012. Social Book Search: Comparing Topical Relevance Judgements and Book Suggestions for Evaluation. In *CIKM'12, October 29–November 2, 2012*. Maui, HI, USA.

Landauer, T. K., McNamara, D. S., Dennis, S., and Kintsch, W. 2007. *Handbook of latent semantic analysis*: Lawrence Erlbaum.

Liu, Yong. 2006. Word of Mouth for Movies: Its Dynamics and Impact on Box Office Revenue. *Journal of Marketing* 70:74-89.

Long, Elizabeth. 2003. *Book clubs: Women and the uses of reading in everyday life*. Chicago: University of Chicago Press.

McDonald, Rónán. 2007. *The death of the critic*. London, New York: Continuum International Publishing Group.

Miall, David S. 2006. *Literary reading: empirical & theoretical studies*. New York: Peter Lang Publishing.

Miller, Donna L. 2011. Talking with Our Fingertips: An Analysis for Habits of Mind in Blogs about Young Adult Books, Arizona State University: PhD.

Mukherjee, Arjun, and Liu, Bing. 2012. Modeling Review Comments. In *Proceedings of 50th Anunal Meeting of Association for Computational Linguistics (ACL-2012)*. Jeju (Korea).

Okanohara, Daisuke, and Tsujii, Jun'ichi. 2005. Assigning polarity scores to reviews using machine learning techniques. *Natural Language Processing–IJCNLP 2005*:314-325.

Pennebaker, J. W., Booth, R. J., and Francis, M. E. 2007. Linguistic Inquiry and Word Count (LIWC2007). Austin, TX.

Pera, Maria Soledad, and Ng, Yiu-Kai. 2011. With a Little Help from My Friends: Generating

Personalized Book Recommendations Using Data Extracted from a Social Website. Paper presented at *Web Intelligence and Intelligent Agent Technology (WI-IAT), 2011*.

Pirmann, Carrie. 2012. Tags in the Catalogue: Insights From a Usability Study of LibraryThing for Libraries. *Library Trends* 61:234-247.

Pool, Gail. 2007. *Faint praise: the plight of book reviewing in America*. Columbia, MO: University of Missouri Press.

Rehberg Sedo, DeNel. 2003. Readers in Reading Groups. An Online Survey of Face-to-Face and Virtual Book Clubs. *Convergence* 9:66-90.

Řehůřek, Radim, and Sojka, Petr. 2010. Software framework for topic modelling with large corpora. Paper presented at *Proceedings of LREC 2010 workshop New Challenges for NLP Frameworks*, Valletta, Malta.

Rosengren, Karl Erik. 1987. Literary criticism: Future invented. *Poetics* 16:295-325.

Steiner, Ann. 2008. Private Criticism in the Public Space: Personal writing on literature in readers' reviews on Amazon. *Participations* 5.

Steiner, Ann. 2010. Personal Readings and Public Texts: Book Blogs and Online Writing about Literature. *Culture unbound* 2:471-494.

Taboada, Maite, Gillies, Mary Ann, and McFetridge, Paul. 2006. Sentiment Classification Techniques for Tracking Literary Reputation. In *Proceedings of LREC 2006 Workshop "Towards Computational Models of Literary Analysis"*.

Taboada, Maite, Brooke, Julian, Tofiloski, Milan, Voll, Kimberly, and Stede, Manfred. 2011. Lexicon-based methods for sentiment analysis. *Computational Linguistics* 37:267-307.

Tsur, Oren, and Rappoport, Ari. 2009. Revrank: A fully unsupervised algorithm for selecting the most helpful book reviews. Paper presented at *International AAAI Conference on Weblogs and Social Media*.

Van Peer, Willie. 2008. Introduction. In *The quality of literature: linguistic studies in literary evaluation*, 1-14. Amsterdam: John Benjamins Publishing Co.

Verboord, Marc. 2010. The Legitimacy of Book Critics in the Age of the Internet and Omnivorousness: Expert Critics, Internet Critics and Peer Critics in Flanders and the Netherlands. *European Sociological Review* 26:623-637.

Verboord, Marc. 2011. Cultural products go online: Comparing the internet and print media on distributions of gender, genre and commercial success. *Communications* 36:441-462.

Von Heydebrand, Renate, and Winko, Simone. 1996. *Einführung in die Wertung von Literatur: Systematik, Geschichte, Legitimation*. Paderborn: Schöningh.

Zijlstra, Hanna, van Meerveld, Tanja, van Middendorp, Henriët, Pennebaker, James W., and Geenen, Rinie. 2004. De Nederlandse versie van de 'Linguistic Inquiry and Word Count' (LIWC). *Gedrag & Gezondheid* 32:271-281.

Clustering voices in *The Waste Land*

Julian Brooke
Dept of Computer Science
University of Toronto
jbrooke@cs.toronto.edu

Graeme Hirst
Dept of Computer Science
University of Toronto
gh@cs.toronto.edu

Adam Hammond
Dept of English
University of Toronto
adam.hammond@utoronto.ca

Abstract

T.S. Eliot's modernist poem *The Waste Land* is often interpreted as collection of voices which appear multiple times throughout the text. Here, we investigate whether we can automatically cluster existing segmentations of the text into coherent, expert-identified characters. We show that clustering *The Waste Land* is a fairly difficult task, though we can do much better than random baselines, particularly if we begin with a good initial segmentation.

1 Introduction

Although literary texts are typically written by a single author, the style of a work of literature is not necessarily uniform. When a certain character speaks, for instance, an author may shift styles to give the character a distinct voice. Typically, voice switches in literature are explicitly marked, either by the use of quotation marks with or without a *said* quotative, or, in cases of narrator switches, by a major textual boundary (e.g. the novel *Ulysses* by James Joyce). However, implicit marking is the norm in some modernist literature: a well-known example is the poem *The Waste Land* by T.S. Eliot, which is usually analyzed in terms of voices that each appear multiple times throughout the text. Our interest is distinguishing these voices automatically.

One of the poem's most distinctive voices is that of the woman who speaks at the end of its second section:

> I can't help it, she said, pulling a long face,
> It's them pills I took, to bring it off, she said
> [158–159]

Her chatty tone and colloquial grammar and lexis distinguish her voice from many others in the poem, such as the formal and traditionally poetic voice of a narrator that recurs many times in the poem:

> Above the antique mantel was displayed
> As though a window gave upon the sylvan scene
> The change of Philomel
> [97–99]

Although the stylistic contrasts between these and other voices are clear to many readers, Eliot does not explicitly mark the transitions, nor is it obvious when a voice has reappeared. Our previous work focused on only the segmentation part of the voice identification task (Brooke et al., 2012). Here, we instead assume an initial segmentation and then try to create clusters corresponding to segments of the *The Waste Land* which are spoken by the same voice. Of particular interest is the influence of the initial segmentation on the success of this downstream task.

2 Related Work

There is a small body of work applying quantitative methods to poetry: Simonton (1990) looked at lexical and semantic diversity in Shakespearean sonnets and correlated this with aesthetic success, whereas Dugan (1973) developed statistics of formulaic style and applied them to the *Chanson de Roland* to determine whether it represents an oral or written style. Kao and Jurafsky (2012) quantify various aspects of poety, including style and sentiment, and use these features to distinguish professional and amateur writers of contemporary poetry.

With respect to novels, the work of McKenna and Antonia (2001) is very relevant; they used principal components analysis of lexical frequency to discriminate different voices and narrative styles in sections of *Ulysses* by James Joyce.

Clustering techniques have been applied to literature in general; for instance, Luyckx (2006) clustered novels according to style, and recent work in distinguishing two authors of sections of the Bible (Koppel et al., 2011) relies crucially on an initial clustering which is bootstrapped into a supervised classifier which is applied to segments. Beyond literature, the tasks of stylistic inconsistency detection (Graham et al., 2005; Guthrie, 2008) and intrinsic (unsupervised) plagiarism detection (Stein et al., 2011) are very closely related to our interests here, though in such tasks usually only two authors are posited; more general kinds of authorship identification (Stamatatos, 2009) may include many more authors, though some form of supervision (i.e. training data) is usually assumed.

Our work here is built on our earlier work (Brooke et al., 2012). Our segmentation model for *The Waste Land* was based on a stylistic change curve whose values are the distance between stylistic feature vectors derived from 50 token spans on either side of each point (spaces between tokens) in the text; the local maxima of this curve represent likely voice switches. Performance on *The Waste Land* was far from perfect, but evaluation using standard text segmentation metrics (Pevzner and Hearst, 2002) indicated that it was well above various baselines.

3 Method

Our approach to voice identification in *The Waste Land* consists first of identifying the boundaries of voice spans (Brooke et al., 2012). Given a segmentation of the text, we consider each span as a data point in a clustering problem. The elements of the vector correspond to the best feature set from the segmentation task, with the rationale that features which were useful for detecting changes in style should also be useful for identifying stylistic similarities. Our features therefore include: a collection of readability metrics (including word length), frequency of punctuation, line breaks, and various parts-of-speech, lexical density, average frequency in a large external corpus (Brants and Franz, 2006), lexicon-based sentiment metrics using SentiWordNet (Baccianella et al., 2010), formality score (Brooke et al., 2010), and, perhaps most notably, the centroid of 20-dimensional distributional vectors built using latent semantic analysis (Landauer and Dumais, 1997), reflecting the use of words in a large web corpus (Burton et al., 2009); in previous work (Brooke et al., 2010), we established that such vectors contain useful stylistic information about the English lexicon (including rare words that appear only occasionally in such a corpus), and indeed LSA vectors were the single most promising feature type for segmentation. For a more detailed discussion of the feature set, see Brooke et al. (2012). All the features are normalized to a mean of zero and a standard deviation of 1.

For clustering, we use a slightly modified version of the popular k-means algorithm (MacQueen, 1967). Briefly, k-means assigns points to a cluster based on their proximity to the k cluster centroids, which are initialized to randomly chosen points from the data and then iteratively refined until convergence, which in our case was defined as a change of less than 0.0001 in the position of each centroid during one iteration.[1] Our version of k-means is distinct in two ways: first, it uses a weighted centroid where the influence of each point is based on the token length of the underlying span, i.e. short (unreliable) spans which fall into the range of some centroid will have less effect on the location of the centroid than larger spans. Second, we use a city-block (L_1) distance function rather than standard Euclidean (L_2) distance function; in the segmentation task, Brooke et al. found that city-block (L1) distance was preferred, a result which is in line with other work in stylistic inconsistency detection (Guthrie, 2008). Though it would be interesting to see if a good k could be estimated independently, for our purposes here we set k to be the known number of speakers in our gold standard.

4 Evaluation

We evaluate our clusters by comparing them to a gold standard annotation. There are various metrics for extrinsic cluster evaluation; Amigó et al.

[1] Occasionally, there was no convergence, at which point we halted the process arbitrarily after 100 iterations.

(2009) review various options and select the BCubed precision and recall metrics (Bagga and Baldwin, 1998) as having all of a set of key desirable properties. BCubed precision is a calculation of the fraction of item pairs in the same cluster which are also in the same category, whereas BCubed recall is the fraction of item pairs in the same category which are also in the same cluster. The harmonic mean of these two metrics is BCubed F-score. Typically, the 'items' are exactly what has been clustered, but this is problematic in our case, because we wish to compare methods which have different segmentations and thus the vectors that are being clustered are not directly comparable. Instead, we calculate the BCubed measures at the level of the token; that is, for the purposes of measuring performance we act as if we had clustered each token individually, instead of the spans of tokens actually used.

Our first evaluation is against a set of 20 artificially-generated 'poems' which are actually randomly generated combinations of parts of 12 poems which were chosen (by an English literature expert, one of the authors) to represent the time period and influences of *The Waste Land*. The longest of these poems is 1291 tokens and the shortest is just 90 tokens (though 10 of the 12 have at least 300 tokens); the average length is 501 tokens. Our method for creating these poems is similar to that of Koppel et al. (2011), though generalized for multiple authors. For each of the artificial poems, we randomly selected 6 poems from the 12 source poems, and then we concatenated 100-200 tokens (or all the remaining tokens, if less than the number selected) from each of these 6 poems to the new combined poem until all the poems were exhausted or below our minimum span length (20 tokens). This allows us to evaluate our method in ideal circumstances, i.e. when there are very distinct voices corresponding to different poets, and the voice spans tend to be fairly long.

Our gold standard annotation of *The Waste Land* speakers is far more tentative. It is based on a number of sources: our own English literature expert, relevant literary analysis (Cooper, 1987), and also *The Waste Land* app (Touch Press LLP, 2011), which includes readings of the poem by various experts, including T.S. Eliot himself. However, there is inherently a great deal of subjectivity involved in literary annotation and, indeed, one of the potential benefits of our work is to find independent justification for a particular voice annotation. Our gold standard thus represents just one potential interpretation of the poem, rather than a true, unique gold standard. The average size of the 69 segments in the gold standard is 50 tokens; the range, however, is fairly wide: the longest is 373 tokens, while the shortest consists of a single token. Our annotation has 13 voices altogether.

We consider three segmentations: the segmentation of our gold standard (Gold), the segmentation predicted by our segmentation model (Automatic), and a segmentation which consists of equal-length spans (Even), with the same number of spans as in the gold standard. The Even segmentation should be viewed as the baseline for segmentation, and the Gold segmentation an "oracle" representing an upper bound on segmentation performance. For the automatic segmentation model, we use the settings from Brooke et al. (2012). We also compare three possible clusterings for each segmentation: no clustering at all (Initial), that is, we assume that each segment is a new voice; k-means clustering (k-means), as outlined above; and random clustering (Random), in which we randomly assign each voice to a cluster. For these latter two methods, which both have a random component, we averaged our metrics over 50 runs. Random and Initial are here, of course, to provide baselines for judging the effectiveness of k-means clustering model. Finally, when using the gold standard segmentation and k-means clustering, we included another oracle option (Seeded): instead of the standard k-means method of randomly choosing them from the available datapoints, each centroid is initialized to the longest instance of a different voice, essentially seeding each cluster.

5 Results

Table 1 contains the results for our first evaluation of voice clustering, the automatically-generated poems. In all the conditions, using the gold segmentation far outstrips the other two options. The automatic segmentation is consistently better than the evenly-spaced baseline, but the performance is actually worse than expected; the segmentation metrics we used in our earlier work

Table 1: Clustering results for artificial poems

Configuration	BCubed metrics		
	Prec.	Rec.	F-score
Initial Even	0.703	0.154	0.249
Initial Automatic	0.827	0.177	0.286
Initial Gold	1.000	0.319	0.465
Random Even	0.331	0.293	0.307
Random Automatic	0.352	0.311	0.327
Random Gold	0.436	0.430	0.436
k-means Even	0.462	0.409	0.430
k-means Automatic	0.532	0.479	0.499
k-means Gold	0.716	0.720	0.710
k-means Gold Seeded	0.869	0.848	0.855

Table 2: Clustering results for *The Waste Land*

Configuration	BCubed metrics		
	Prec.	Rec.	F-score
Initial Even	0.792	0.069	0.128
Initial Automatic	0.798	0.084	0.152
Initial Gold	1.000	0.262	0.415
Random Even	0.243	0.146	0.183
Random Automatic	0.258	0.160	0.198
Random Gold	0.408	0.313	0.352
k-means Even	0.288	0.238	0.260
k-means Automatic	0.316	0.264	0.296
k-means Gold	0.430	0.502	0.461
k-means Gold Seeded	0.491	0.624	0.550

The results for *The Waste Land* are in Table 2. Many of the basic patterns are the same, including the consistent ranking of the methods; overall, however, the clustering is far less effective. This is particularly true for the gold-standard condition, which only increases modestly between the initial and clustered state; the marked increase in recall is balanced by a major loss of precision. In fact, unlike with the artificial text, the most promising aspect of the clustering seems to be the fairly sizable boost to the quality of clusters in automatic segmenting performance. The effect of seeding is also very consistent, nearly as effective as in the automatic case.

We also looked at the results for individual speakers in *The Waste Land*; many of the speakers (some of which appear only in a few lines) are very poorly distinguished, even with the gold-standard segmentation and seeding, but there are a few that cluster quite well; the best two are in fact our examples from Section 1,[2] that is, the narrator (F-score 0.869), and the chatty woman (F-score 0.605). The former result is particularly important, from the perspective of literary analysis, since there are several passages which seem to be the main narrator (and our expert annotated them as such) but which are definitely open to interpretation.

6 Conclusion

Literature, by its very nature, involves combining existing means of expression in surprising new ways, resisting supervised analysis methods that depend on assumptions of conformity. Our unsupervised approach to distinguishing voices in poetry offers this necessary flexibility, and indeed seems to work reasonably well in cases when the stylistic differences are clear. *The Waste Land*, however, is a very subtle text, and our results suggest that we are a long way from something that would be a considered a possible human interpretation. Nevertheless, applying quantitative methods to these kinds of texts can, for literary scholars, bridge the gab between abstract interpretations and the details of form and function (McKenna and Antonia, 2001). In our own case, this computational work is just one aspect of a larger project in literary analysis where the ultimate goal is not to mimic human behavior per se, but rather to better understand literary phenomena by annotation and modelling of these phenomena (Hammond, 2013; Hammond et al., 2013).

With respect to future enhancements, improving segmentation is obviously important; the best automated efforts so far provide only a small boost over a baseline approach to segmentation. However, independently of this, our experiments with gold-standard seeding suggest that refining our approach to clustering, e.g. a method that identifies good initial points for our centroids, may also pay dividends in the long run. A more radical idea for future work would be to remove the somewhat artificial delim-

[2]These passages are the original examples from our earlier work (Brooke et al., 2012), selected by our expert for their distinctness, so the fact that they turned out to be the most easily clustered is actually a result of sorts (albeit an anecdotal one), suggesting that our clustering behavior does correspond somewhat to a human judgment of distinctness.

itation of the task into segmentation and clustering phases, building a model which works iteratively to produce segments that are sensitive to points of stylistic change but that, at a higher level, also form good clusters (as measured by intrinsic measures of cluster quality).

Acknowledgements

This work was financially supported by the Natural Sciences and Engineering Research Council of Canada.

References

Enrique Amigó, Julio Gonzalo, Javier Artiles, and Felisa Verdejo. 2009. A comparison of extrinsic clustering evaluation metrics based on formal constraints. *Information Retrieval*, 12:461–486, August.

Stefano Baccianella, Andrea Esuli, and Fabrizio Sebastiani. 2010. SentiWordNet 3.0: An enhanced lexical resource for sentiment analysis and opinion mining. In *Proceedings of the 7th Conference on International Language Resources and Evaluation (LREC'10)*, Valletta, Malta, May.

Amit Bagga and Breck Baldwin. 1998. Entity-based cross-document coreferencing using the vector space model. In *Proceedings of the 36th Annual Meeting of the Association for Computational Linguistics and 17th International Conference on Computational Linguistics (ACL-COLING '98)*, pages 79–85, Montreal, Quebec, Canada.

Thorsten Brants and Alex Franz. 2006. *Web 1T 5-gram Corpus Version 1.1.* Google Inc.

Julian Brooke, Tong Wang, and Graeme Hirst. 2010. Automatic acquisition of lexical formality. In *Proceedings of the 23rd International Conference on Computational Linguistics (COLING '10)*, Beijing.

Julian Brooke, Adam Hammond, and Graeme Hirst. 2012. Unsupervised stylistic segmentation of poetry with change curves and extrinsic features. In *Proceedings of the 1st Workshop on Computational Literature for Literature (CLFL '12)*, Montreal.

Kevin Burton, Akshay Java, and Ian Soboroff. 2009. The ICWSM 2009 Spinn3r Dataset. In *Proceedings of the Third Annual Conference on Weblogs and Social Media (ICWSM 2009)*, San Jose, CA.

John Xiros Cooper. 1987. *T.S. Eliot and the politics of voice: The argument of The Waste Land.* UMI Research Press, Ann Arbor, Mich.

Joseph J. Duggan. 1973. *The Song of Roland: Formulaic style and poetic craft.* University of California Press.

Neil Graham, Graeme Hirst, and Bhaskara Marthi. 2005. Segmenting documents by stylistic character. *Natural Language Engineering*, 11(4):397–415.

David Guthrie. 2008. *Unsupervised Detection of Anomalous Text.* Ph.D. thesis, University of Sheffield.

Adam Hammond, Julian Brooke, and Graeme Hirst. 2013. A tale of two cultures: Bringing literary analysis and computational linguistics together. In *Proceedings of the 2nd Workshop on Computational Literature for Literature (CLFL '13)*, Atlanta.

Adam Hammond. 2013. He do the police in different voices: Looking for voices in *The Waste Land*. Seminar: "Mapping the Fictional Voice" American Comparative Literature Association (ACLA).

Justine Kao and Dan Jurafsky. 2012. A computational analysis of style, sentiment, and imagery in contemporary poetry. In *Proceedings of the 1st Workshop on Computational Literature for Literature (CLFL '12)*, Montreal.

Moshe Koppel, Navot Akiva, Idan Dershowitz, and Nachum Dershowitz. 2011. Unsupervised decomposition of a document into authorial components. In *Proceedings of the 49th Annual Meeting of the Association for Computational Linguistics (ACL '11)*, Portland, Oregon.

Thomas K. Landauer and Susan Dumais. 1997. A solution to Plato's problem: The latent semantic analysis theory of the acquisition, induction, and representation of knowledge. *Psychological Review*, 104:211–240.

Kim Luyckx, Walter Daelemans, and Edward Vanhoutte. 2006. Stylogenetics: Clustering-based stylistic analysis of literary corpora. In *Proceedings of the 5th International Conference on Language Resources and Evaluation (LREC '06)*, Genoa, Italy.

J. B. MacQueen. 1967. Some methods for classification and analysis of multivariate observations. In *Proceedings of the Fifth Berkeley Symposium on Mathematical Statistics and Probability*, pages 281–297.

C. W. F. McKenna and A. Antonia. 2001. The statistical analysis of style: Reflections on form, meaning, and ideology in the 'Nausicaa' episode of *Ulysses*. *Literary and Linguistic Computing*, 16(4):353–373.

Lev Pevzner and Marti A. Hearst. 2002. A critique and improvement of an evaluation metric for text segmentation. *Computational Linguistics*, 28:19–36, March.

Dean Keith Simonton. 1990. Lexical choices and aesthetic success: A computer content analysis of 154 Shakespeare sonnets. *Computers and the Humanities*, 24(4):251–264.

Efstathios Stamatatos. 2009. A survey of modern authorship attribution methods. *Journal of the American Society for Information Science and Technology*, 60(3):538–556.

Benno Stein, Nedim Lipka, and Peter Prettenhofer. 2011. Intrinsic plagiarism analysis. *Language Resources and Evaluation*, 45(1):63–82.

Touch Press LLP. 2011. *The Waste Land* app. http://itunes.apple.com/ca/app/the-waste-land/id427434046?mt=8 .

An initial study of topical poetry segmentation

Chris Fournier
University of Ottawa
Ottawa, ON, Canada
cfour037@eecs.uottawa.ca

Abstract

This work performs some basic research upon topical poetry segmentation in a pilot study designed to test some initial assumptions and methodologies. Nine segmentations of the poem titled Kubla Khan (Coleridge, 1816, pp. 55-58) are collected and analysed, producing low but comparable inter-coder agreement. Analyses and discussions of these codings focus upon how to improve agreement and outline some initial results on the nature of topics in this poem.

1 Introduction

Topical segmentation is the division of a text by placing boundaries between segments. Within a segmentation, each segment should represent a coherent and cohesive topic. The decision to place a boundary between two segments of text is subjective and must often be determined manually. The factors involved in performing this subjective task are poorly understood, which motivates this work to begin the basic research required to understand this phenomenon.

For literature, topical segmentations have been produced for a short story (Kozima, 1993) and a novel (Kazantseva and Szpakowicz, 2012). Poetry, however, has had little attention in terms of topical segmentation. Brooke et al. (2012) collected segmentations of poetry that sought to delineate which voices communicate various segments of *The Wasteland* by T.S. Elliot (1888-1965), but a voice segment does not necessarily correlate with a topical segment. Because *The Wasteland*'s defining feature is its voice-shifts, more data is required to understand the variety of topical segments that could exist within poetry besides those delineated by changing voice — which this work aims to provide.[1]

[1] Available at http://nlp.chrisfournier.ca/

This work's goal is to begin to provide some initial information about what constitutes a topic in poetry by analysing the Romantic-era poem titled *Kubla Khan* (Coleridge, 1816, pp. 55-58) by Samuel Taylor Coleridge (1772–1834). Chosen for its beauty, variety, short length (54 lines), and lack of strict adherence to a prescribed structure (e.g., sonnets, odes, etc.), it is assumed that this purported fragment of a dream will contain a wide variety of different topics (as judged by manual coders).

This work aims to discover from reader's interpretations of topical segmentation in poetry the:

- Structure of these topics (e.g., are they linear, hierarchical, or something else?);
- Types and variety of topics (e.g., do topics shift when there are changes in time, place, description, exposition, etc.); and
- Relationship between poetic features and topical boundaries (e.g., do stanzas correlate with topical boundaries?).

Unfortunately, this work is simply a pilot study and it cannot make any generalizations about poetry overall, but inferences can be made about this single poem and its topical structure.

2 Related Work

Topical Segmentation Topical segmentation of expository texts such as popular science magazine articles have been well studied by Hearst (1993, 1994, 1997) while developing the automatic topical segmenter named *TextTiling*. On a parallel track, Kozima (1993) segmented a simplified version of O. Henry's (William Sydney Porter; 1862–1910) short story titled *Springtime à la Carte* (Thornley, 1816). Both bodies of work focused upon using lexical cohesion to model where topic boundaries occur and collected manual segmentations to study. This data, however, was never analysed for the types of segments contained, but only for the presence or absence of topic boundaries at specific positions.

Kazantseva and Szpakowicz (2012) delved deeper into topical segmentation of literature by collecting segmentations of Wilkie Collins' (1824–1883) romantic novel *The Moonstone* (Collins, 1868). In the novel, 20 of its chapters were segmented individually by 27 annotators (in groups of 4–6) into episodes. Episodes were defined as "topically continuous spans of text demarcated by the most perceptible shifts of topic in the chapter" (Kazantseva and Szpakowicz, 2012, p. 213). This work also analysed the boundaries placed by the coders themselves, but not the types of segments that they produced.

Brooke et al. (2012) collected voice-switch segmentations of *The Wasteland* by T.S. Elliot (1888-1965). Although voices are not topics, voice switching could constitute topical boundaries. Segmentations from 140 English literature undergraduate students and 6 expert readings were collected and used to compose one authoritative reference segmentation to test a large number automatic segmenters upon.

Agreement and Comparison Inter-coder agreement coefficients measure the agreement between a group of human judges (i.e. coders) and whether their agreement is greater than chance. Low coefficient values indicate that a task may have restricted coders such that their responses do not represent an empirical model of the task, or the task instructions did not sufficiently define the task. High coefficient values indicate the degree of reliability and replicability of a coding scheme and the coding collection methodology (Carletta, 1996). Although there is much debate about what coefficient value represents adequate agreement, any coefficient value can be used to compare studies of the same task that use different coding schemes or methodologies.

Many inter-coder agreement coefficients exist, but this work uses Fleiss' multi-π (π^*, Fleiss 1971; occasionally referred to as K by Siegel and Castellan 1988) to measure agreement because it generalizes individual coder performance to give a better picture of the replicability of a study. Specifically, an adaptation of the proposal by Fournier and Inkpen (2012, pp. 154–156) for computing π^* is used that is detailed by Fournier (2013).

Fournier (2013) modifies the work of Fournier and Inkpen (2012) to provide a more discriminative measure of similarity between segmentations called *boundary similarity* (B) — an edit distance based measure which is unbiased, more consistent, and more intuitive than traditional segmentation comparison methods such as P_k (Beeferman and Berger, 1999, pp. 198–200) and WindowDiff (Pevzner and Hearst, 2002, p. 10). Using the inter-coder agreement formulations provided in Fournier and Inkpen (2012), Fournier (2013) provides B-based inter-coder agreement coefficients including Fleiss' multi-π (referred to as π^*_{B}) which can discern between low/high agreement while still awarding partial credit for near misses.

3 Study Design

This work is a small study meant to inform future larger studies on topical poetry segmentation. To that end, a single 54 line poem, *Kubla Khan* (Coleridge, 1816, pp. 55-58), is segmented. Written in four stanzas (originally published in two) composed of tetra and penta-meter iambs, this well studied work appears to show a large variety of topical segment breaks, including time, place, scenery, narration, exposition, etc. Stripped of its indentation and with its stanzas compressed into one long sequence of numbered lines, this poem was presented to segmenters to divide into topics.

Objectives The objective of this study is to identify whether topics in poems fit well into a linear topic structure (i.e., boundaries cannot overlap) and to test the annotation instructions used. Additionally, a survey of the types and variety of topics is desirable to inform whether more than one boundary type might be needed to model segment boundaries (and to inspire statistical features for training an automatic topical poetry segmenter). Finally, the relationship between poem features and topic boundaries is of interest; specifically, for this initial work, do stanzas correlate with topical boundaries?

Subjects Nine subjects were recruited using Amazon's Mechanical Turk from the United States who had an exemplary work record (i.e., were "Master Tukers"). Segment text summaries were analysed for correct language use to ensure that coders demonstrated English language proficiency.

Granularity Segmentations were solicited at the line level (arbitrarily assuming that a topic will not change within a line, but may between lines). This level is assumed to be fine enough to partition segments accurately while still being coarse enough to make the task short (only 54 lines can be divided into segments). Because there may be a great number of topics found in the poem by readers, it is assumed that a nearly missed boundary would only be those that are adjacent to another (i.e., n_t for B is set to 2).

Collection procedure Segmenters were asked to read the poem and to divide it into topical segments where a topic boundary could represent a change in time, scenery, or any other detail that the reader deems important. A short example coding was also provided to augment the instructions. Along with line number spans, a single sentence description of the segment was requested (for segment type analysis and to verify coder diligence and thoughtfulness) and overall comments on the task were solicited.

4 Study Results and Analysis

Time The 9 subjects took 35.1556 ± 18.6796 minutes to read and segment the poem.[2] Each was remunerated \$8 USD, or $\$18.91 \pm 11.03$ USD per hour.

Segmentations The 9 coders placed 17.6667 ± 6.2716 boundaries within the 54 lines of the poem. The number of segmentations produced by each coder is shown in Figure 1a, along with the mean and standard deviation (SD).

Agreement The segmentations provided by the 9 coders in this study have an inter-coder agreement coefficient value of $\pi^*_{\text{B}} = 0.3789$. This value is low, but it is only slightly below that of Hearst (1997) (0.4405) and Kazantseva and Szpakowicz (2012) (0.20, 0.18, 0.40, 0.38, 0.23 for each of the 5 groups) as reported in Fournier (2013). This value is also not unexpected given the different coding behaviours (e.g., boundary placement frequency) in Figure 1a.

Similarity Using Boundary Similarity (B), taking $1 - \text{B}$ can yield a simple distance function between segmentations. Because of the low agreement of this study, it is assumed that there must be subsets of coders who agree more with each other than with others (i.e., clusters). Using $1-\text{B}$ as a distance function between segmentations, hierarchical agglomerative clustering was used to obtain the clusters shown in Figure 1b. Computing inter-coder agreement for these clusters produces subsets with significantly higher than overall agreement (Table 1).

Labels Taking the single-sentence descriptions of each topic, an attempt was made to label them as belonging to one or more of these categories:

1. Exposition (e.g, story/plot development);
2. Event (e.g., an action or event occurred);
3. Place (Location is stated or changed);
4. Description (of an entity; can be specific): *a*) Scenery *b*) Person *c*) Sound *d*) Comparison (simile or metaphor)
5. Statement (to the reader).

These labels were decided by the author while reading the segmentations and were iteratively constructed until they suitably described the one-line segment topic summaries. Using Jaccard similarity, the labels placed on each position were compared to those of each other coder to obtain mean similarity of each line, as plotted in Figure 1c. This shows that in terms of topic types, actual agreement varies by position. The portions with the highest agreement are at the beginning of the poem and contain scenery description which appear to have been easy to agree upon (type-wise). Overall, mean label similarity between all coders was 0.5330 ± 0.4567, but some of the identified clusters exhibited even higher similarity (Table 1).

Feature correlations There is some evidence to suggest that boundaries between the four stanzas at lines 11–12, 30–31, and 36–37 correlate with topical shifts because $^6/_9$, $^9/_9$, and $^9/_9$ (respectively) coders placed boundaries at these locations. There is little evidence to suggest that the indentation of line 5 and lines 31–34 (not shown) correlate with topical shifts because only $^1/_9$ and $^5/_9$ (respectively) coders placed boundaries between these segments.

Topical structure One of the coders commented that they felt that the segments should overlap and

[2] One coder took far less time because they submitted part of their answers via email and time was not accurately recorded.

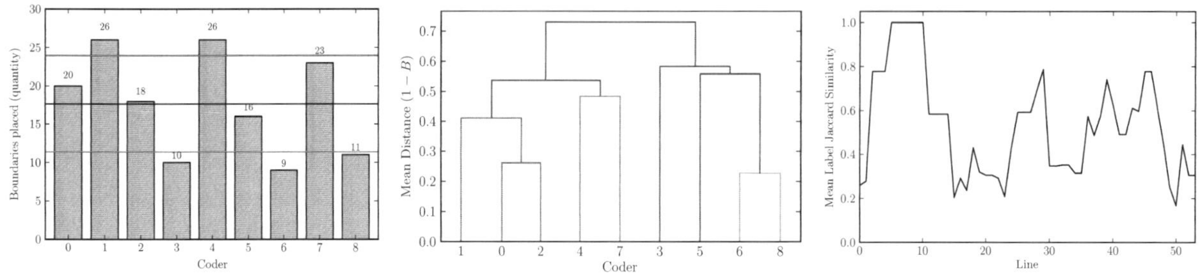

(a) Coder boundaries placed with mean and SD

(b) Hierarchical agglomerative clusters using 1 − B as a distance metric

(c) Mean Jaccard similarity of topic label types per line

Figure 1: Various analyses of the 9 manual segmentations of Kubla Khan

Coders	$\{4,7\}$	$\{0,2\}$	$\{6,8\}$	$\{1,0,2\}$	$\{1,0,2,4,7\}$	$\{3,5,6,8\}$	$\{5,6,8\}$
π^*_B	0.3704	0.6946	0.7625	0.5520	0.4474	0.4764	0.5389
E(J)	0.491 ± 0.495	0.460 ± 0.439	0.685 ± 0.464	0.508 ± 0.452	0.512 ± 0.467	0.593 ± 0.425	0.580 ± 0.432

Table 1: Inter-coder agreement (π^*_B) and mean Jaccard topic label similarity (with WD) for coder clusters

coded so. These codings were adjusted by the author to not overlap for analysis, but the coder's comment highlights that perhaps these segments should be able to overlap, or that linear segmentation may not be an adequate model for topics in poetry.

5 Discussion

Given the low (but comparable) inter-coder agreement values of this study, it is evident that some variables are not properly being controlled by the procedure used herein. Before a larger study is performed, the issue of low agreement must be explained; some hypotheses for this are that:

1. Coders may have been of varying levels of education, English proficiency, or motivation;
2. Instructions may have not been clear or exhaustive in terms of the potential topics types;
3. A linear segmentation not allowing for overlap may artificially constrain coders; and
4. The poem selected may simply be inherently difficult to interpret and thus segment.

This study has, however, catalogued a number of topic labels which can be used to better educate coders about the types of topical segments that exist, which could lead to obtaining higher inter-coder agreement. Pockets of agreement do exist, as shown in the clusters and their agreement and topic label similarity values (Table 1). If more data is collected, but inter-coder agreement stays steady, perhaps instead these clusters will remain and become more populated. Maybe these clusters will reveal that the problem was modelled correctly, but that there is simply a difference between the coders that was not previously known. Such a difference could be spotted using clustering, but what the actual difference is may remain a mystery unless more biographical details are available (e.g., sex, age, education, English proficiency, reading preferences, etc.).

6 Conclusions and Future Work

Although Kubla Khan is a beautiful poem, its topical segmentation is vexing. Low inter-coder agreement exemplified by this study indicates that the methodology used to investigate topical poetry segmentation may require some modifications, or more biographical details must be sought to identify the cause of the low agreement. Clustering was able to identify pockets of high agreement and similarity, but the nature of these clusters is largely unknown — what biographical details or subjective opinions of the task separate these groups?

Future work will continue with subsequent pilot studies to attempt to raise the level of inter-coder agreement or to explain the low agreement by looking for clusters of coders who agree (and attempting to explain the relationships between coders in these clusters). Also, more poems need to be analysed to make generalisations about poetry overall. The relationships between topical segments in poetry and other poetic features such as rhyme, meter, and expert opinions are also worth investigation.

References

Beeferman, Doug and Adam Berger. 1999. Statistical models for text segmentation. *Machine Learning* 34:177–210.

Brooke, Julian, Adam Hammond, and Graeme Hirst. 2012. Unsupervised Stylistic Segmentation of Poetry with Change Curves and Extrinsic Features. In *Proceedings of the 1st NAACL-HLT Workshop on Computational Linguistics for Literature*. Association for Computational Linguistics, Stroudsburg, PA, USA, pages 26–35.

Carletta, Jean. 1996. Assessing Agreement on Classification Tasks: The Kappa Statistic. *Computational Linguistics* 22(2):249–254.

Coleridge, Samuel Taylor. 1816. *Christabel, Kubla Khan, and the Pains of Sleep*. John Murray.

Collins, Wilkie. 1868. *The Moonstone*. Tinsley Brothers.

Fleiss, Joseph L. 1971. Measuring nominal scale agreement among many raters. *Psychological Bulletin* 76:378–382.

Fournier, Chris. 2013. Evaluating Text Segmentation using Boundary Edit Distance. In *Proceedings of 51st Annual Meeting of the Association for Computational Linguistics*. Association for Computational Linguistics, Stroudsburg, PA, USA.

Fournier, Chris and Diana Inkpen. 2012. Segmentation Similarity and Agreement. In *Proceedings of Human Language Technologies: The 2012 Annual Conference of the North American Chapter of the Association for Computational Linguistics*. Association for Computational Linguistics, Stroudsburg, PA, USA, pages 152–161.

Hearst, Marti A. 1993. TextTiling: A Quantitative Approach to Discourse. Technical report, University of California at Berkeley, Berkeley, CA, USA.

Hearst, Marti A. 1994. *Context and Structured in Automated Full-Text Information Access Context and Structure in Automated Full-Text Information Access*. Ph.D. thesis, University of California Berkeley.

Hearst, Marti A. 1997. TextTiling: Segmenting Text into Multi-paragraph Subtopic Passages. *Computational Linguistics* 23:33–64.

Kazantseva, Anna and Stan Szpakowicz. 2012. Topical Segmentation: a Study of Human Performance. In *Proceedings of Human Language Technologies: The 2012 Annual Conference of the North American Chapter of the Association for Computational Linguistics*. Association for Computational Linguistics, Stroudsburg, PA, USA, pages 211–220.

Kozima, Hideki. 1993. Text segmentation based on similarity between words. In *Proceedings of the 31st Annual Meeting of the Association for Computational Linguistics*. Association for Computational Linguistics, Stroudsburg, PA, USA, ACL '93, pages 286–288.

Pevzner, Lev and Marti A. Hearst. 2002. A critique and improvement of an evaluation metric for text segmentation. *Computational Linguistics* 28:19–36.

Siegel, Sidney and N. J. Castellan. 1988. *Nonparametric Statistics for the Behavioral Sciences*, McGraw-Hill, New York, USA, chapter 9.8. 2 edition.

Thornley, G. C., editor. 1816. *British and American Short Stories*. Longman Simplified English Series. Longman.

Groundhog DAG: Representing Semantic Repetition in Literary Narratives*

Greg Lessard
French Studies
Queen's University
Canada
greg.lessard@queensu.ca

Michael Levison
School of Computing
Queen's University
Canada
levison@cs.queensu.ca

Abstract

This paper discusses the concept of *semantic repetition* in literary texts, that is, the recurrence of elements of meaning, possibly in the absence of repeated formal elements. A typology of semantic repetition is presented, as well as a framework for analysis based on the use of threaded Directed Acyclic Graphs. This model is applied to the script for the movie *Groundhog Day*. It is shown first that semantic repetition presents a number of traits not found in the case of the repetition of formal elements (letters, words, etc.). Consideration of the threaded DAG also brings to light several classes of semantic repetition, between individual nodes of a DAG, between subDAGs within a larger DAG, and between structures of subDAGs, both within and across texts. The model presented here provides a basis for the detailed study of additional literary texts at the semantic level and illustrates the tractability of the formalism used for analysis of texts of some considerable length and complexity.

1 Background

Repetition, that is, the reuse of a finite number of elements, is a fundamental characteristic of natural language. Thus, the words of a language are composed of a small number of phonemes or letters, sentences are constructed from repeated words, as well as larger collocational or syntactic chunks, and so on. Most work on repetition has been concerned with the study of such recurring formal elements, typically from the perspective of their frequency. However, it is important to recognize that a text can present not only cases in which some form recurs, as in 1(a) below, but also instances where meaning recurs, without any formal element being necessarily repeated, as in 1(b).

(1) (a) Brutus has *killed* Caesar! He has *killed* him!

(b) Brutus has *killed* Caesar! He *plunged his knife into him and our beloved leader is dead!*

It is such *semantic repetition* that concerns us here: that is, the repetition of some semantic content within a text, without there being necessarily a formal element which recurs. In particular, we wish to study semantic repetition in literary texts. This is important, since literature often brings with it the expectation that repetition is significant. To put this another way, repetition tends to be *semanticized*: its very existence 'means' something. Consider this first at the formal level. It is well-known that human language processing tends to extract meaning from sequences of forms and retain the forms themselves for only a limited time. Literary texts counteract this fading effect by several linguistic means, including physical proximity of repeated items, stress, and syntactic position. Devices such as these often carry additional information on importance or some other factor, as when an orator repeats the same word or sequence. This has been much discussed. To mention several examples among many, Jakobson (1960) refers to this as the *poetic function* of language, Genette (1972) provides a typology of narrative repetition, Tsur (2008) argues

*This research was supported in part by the Social Sciences and Humanities Research Council of Canada.

that repetition is one of the devices which 'slows down' processing of text and contributes to poetic effects, Tannen (1989) gives examples of the usage of repetition in oral discourse, Okpewho (1992) shows its importance in folk literature, and Johnstone (1991) examines the role of repetition in Arabic discourse.

As we will see below, semantic repetition in literature also lends itself to semanticization. In other words, the fact that events are repeated in a narrative can be, and often is, seen not as the product of chance but rather as part of a larger pattern. The potential for this is supported by several features of meaning. First, as Stanhope et al. (1993) have shown in their work on the long-term retention of a novel, unlike formal elements, at least some semantic elements are extremely resistant to decay and can be recalled weeks and even many months later. As a result, the fading effects observed earlier for formal repetition cannot be assumed to apply in exactly the same fashion to semantic repetition: items remain accessible across entire texts and even across different texts. Second, there is in principle no upper limit on the size of semantic elements which may be repeated. At one extreme, a single character from a novel may remain in memory, along with some of the items associated with him or her. If one hears the single word *Hamlet*, what comes to mind? At the other, entire plots may be recalled. If asked to summarize the plot of *A Christmas Carol* in 100 words, most native speakers would have no difficulty in doing this. And third, by their tendency to exploit and semanticize repetition, literary texts differ from other genres, such as expository texts, whose goal is typically to present some set of information in a coherent fashion such that the same element *not* be repeated.

In light of this, our goal here is threefold: to give a sense of the diversity of semantic repetition in literary texts, including its various granularities; to propose a formal model capable of dealing with these various dimensions of semantic repetition; and to test this model against an actual text of some considerable length.

2 Events and repetition

Let us assume for the moment that semantic repetition is limited to repeated *events*, leaving aside issues of repeated qualities, entities and so on. A number of formal and semantic tools suggest themselves for dealing with this case. Within a single utterance, a neo-Davidsonian event semantics might be used, as shown in (2), where *e* represents the 'glue' which ties together the action and the agent.

$$\exists e[speak(e) \wedge agent(e) = fred(e)] \quad (2)$$

This places the event at the centre of focus. The logical machinery behind this has been extended in various ways. For example, Hewitt (2012) proposes the use of *serial logic* to capture ordered sets of events. In addition, since events are also repeated across utterances and related to other events, as in conversations, Asher and Lascarides (2003) provides an extended logical formalism to begin to deal with this and Helbig (2006) proposes several specific functions for linking propositions, including `CAUS` (causality), `CONTR` (contrast), and `CONF` (conformity with an abstract frame). However, both approaches are applied to short spans of text and neither deals explicitly with repetition.

At a slightly higher level of granularity, Rhetorical Structure Theory (Mann and Thompson, 1988) provides a set of frameworks to describe relationships among elements of a paragraph, some of which, `Restatement` and `Elaboration` in particular, have the potential to deal with elements of repetition.[1] Work in Natural Language Generation, which has often focused on the production of longer expository texts, has also typically paid more attention to the reduction of repetition than to its production.[2] Even work on narrative generation has tended to concentrate mostly on reduction of repetition (Callaway and Lester, 2001; Callaway and Lester, 2002).

Several attempts have been made to deal with longer spans of texts, typically based on the markup of elements within a text. Most recently, Mani (2012) proposes a *Narrative Markup Language* capable of dealing with elements of repetition, but this markup is anchored to the text itself and it is unclear how such an approach could capture more abstract elements of semantic repetition. In fact, the fundamental issue

[1] For details, see `http://www.sfu.ca/rst/01intro/definitions.html`.

[2] See, however, de Rosis and Grasso (2000) who argue for the role of what they call *redundancy*.

is that semantic repetition exists across a wide range of spans, from the very smallest (both across different events and within elements of some inherently repeated activity (Tovena and Donazzan, 2008)), to the very largest, spanning multiple texts. To illustrate this, consider the following cases.

(a) A single event and the memory of the event in the mind of the perpetrator. For example, Brutus stabs Caesar, and then the next day replays the stabbing in his memory.

(b) A single event seen from the point of view of two different characters. For example, Livia sees Brutus stab Caesar, and so does Cassius.

(c) A single, perhaps complex, event, whose different facets are represented, perhaps in an interspersed fashion. Good examples of this are found in cinema, such as Eisenstein's famous bridge scene in *October*, or the Odessa steps scene in *Battleship Potemkin*, where the same images recur (such as the opening bridge, the dead horse, or the baby carriage tipping on the end of a stairway).

Examples such as these illustrate what might be called *representational repetition*, in which the same (perhaps complex) event is shown from different points of view. However, we also find examples of what might be called *class-based repetition*, in which various simple examples share a common abstract structure, as the following examples illustrate.

(d) Two sets of events in the same text represent instantiations of the same *topos*, or recurring narrative structure. For example, the Hebrew Bible contains multiple instances in which a parent favours a younger sibling over an older one. Thus, the Deity favours Abel over Cain, Abraham favours Isaac over Ishmael, Isaac favours Jacob over Esau, and so on. In these cases, we are actually faced with an abstract framework which is instantiated with different actual parameters.

(e) Two different texts represent the same abstract plot. Thus, *Pyramus and Thisbe* and *Romeo and Juliet* may both be represented by the same abstract formula, which we captures the story of star-crossed lovers whose feuding families lead to their demise.

Examples such as (d) and (e) show that at least some elements of literary repetition may only be captured by some device which permits a greater degree of abstraction than is provided by traditional devices like predicate calculus or instance-based markup. From the literary perspective, they are sometimes referred to as *topoi*, that is, recurring narrative sequences.[3] However, as formulated in most literary analyses, the notion of topos has several shortcomings. First, definitions tend to be informal.[4] Second, the granularity of topoi is unclear. One might express a given topos in very general terms or quite specifically.

Our goal here is to build on the insights of literary theory regarding the *meaning* of literary texts, while retaining some level of formalism. To do this, we need first to respect the empirical richness of literary texts. As the examples above show, simple two-line examples are not sufficient to show the true complexity of semantic repetition. Accordingly, we have chosen as our corpus an entire movie script, described below. Second, in the case of semantic repetition, we need a formalism capable of captureing various levels of granularity, from quite fine to very general, and which shows not just differences of point of view, but elements of class inclusion. To do accomplish this, we have adopted the formalism described in Levison et al. (2012), based on a functional representation of meaning elements by means of *semantic expressions*.[5] When combined with the use of threaded Directed Acyclic Graphs, discussed below, this formalism permits the representation of elements of meaning at various levels of granularity,

3 *Groundhog Day*

To illustrate the phenomenon of semantic repetition, we have created a formal analysis of the screenplay for the popular movie *Groundhog Day* (henceforth,

[3]A detailed list of topoi, together with examples, may be found in `http://satorbase.org`.

[4]See Lessard et al. (2004) for one attempt at formalization. Note also that the concept of topos shares features with the concept of *scripts* (Schank and Abelson, 1977), which has been formalized to some degree.

[5]The formalism is inspired by the Haskell programming language (Bird, 1998).

GH).[6] Because of its plot structure, discussed below, the script represents arguably an extreme case of semantic repetition and thus a good test of the proposed model of semantic repetition.

GH recounts the story of Phil Connors, an egocentric weatherman, who has been sent with his producer, Rita, and cameraman Larry, to cover the annual February 2 event at Punxsutawney, Pennsylvania, where a groundhog (Punxsutawney Phil), by seeing or not seeing his shadow, provides a prediction on the number of weeks remaining in winter. Displeased at such a lowly assignment, Connors behaves badly to all. However, on waking up the next day, he discovers that it is still February 2, and the day unfolds as it had previously. In the many subsequent iterations of the day, Connors discovers the possibilities inherent in there being no consequences to his acts, the advantages of being able to perfect the elements of a seduction by repeated trials, and finally, the value of altruism and love. At this point, after many iterations, the cycle is broken, and Phil and Rita, now in love, greet February 3.[7]

4 Directed Acyclic Graphs

To capture the various elements of granularity in the GH script, we make use of the well-known distinction in literary theory between two perspectives on a narrative. The *fabula* or *histoire* is the information on which the narrative is based; the *sjuzhet* or *récit* is a particular telling (Bal, 1985; Genette, 1983). In our model, we represent the former, which we shall term a *story*, by a *Directed Acyclic Graph*, henceforth DAG. A directed graph is a collection of nodes linked by unidirectional paths. In an acyclic graph, no sequence of paths may link back to a node already visited. In technical terms, the dependency relation portrayed by the graph is transitive, irreflexive and antisymmetric. Within the DAG, nodes denote pieces of the meaning, perhaps at different levels of granularity, and directed paths which indicate the dependence of one node upon another. By dependence, we mean that subsequent nodes in the DAG make use of information present on previous nodes. In a finer analysis, the nature of the various dependencies might be sub-divided into subclasses like logical dependency, temporal dependency, and so on, but we will not do that here.

As noted earlier, we represent the meanings carried by the nodes of a DAG by means of *semantic expressions*. So, for example, given the semantic entities `phil` and `rita`, and the action `meet`, the expression `meet(phil, rita)` represents a meeting between the two characters in the film. This expression represents what is called, in the framework used, a *completion*. Although the functional representation used permits the representation of semantic niceties like temporal relations and definiteness, the model used here does not include them. In the analysis here, each semantic expression corresponds to one node of the DAG. Of course, such a model may vary in granularity. At one extreme, the entire script could be represented by a single expression (as in `improve(phil)`. At the other, each small event could form the basis of a semantic expression. For the purposes of the present analysis, we have adopted an intermediate granularity.[8]

Each element of the functional representation is drawn from a *semantic lexicon* composed of a formal specification and an informal one, which provides a basic-level textual output, as shown by the following examples:

```
meet :: (entity, entity)
     -> completion
meet(x,y) =
     "[x] meets [y]"
```

where the first line shows the formal specification and the second line the informal one. The sequence of semantic expressions, when used to call the informal representations, thus provides the gist of the script, or alternatively, can be used to drive a natural language generation environment. In addition, since the elements of the DAG are formally specified in the semantic lexicon, they may be analyzed or further manipulated by graph manipulation software. To take a trivial case, the transitive closure of a DAG might be calculated.

[6] It should be noted that this screenplay, which may be found online at `http://www.dailyscript.com/scripts/groundhogday.pdf`, diverges in some respects from the film. It contains some scenes which do not appear in the film, and it does not contain some others which do appear in the film.

[7] A fuller synopsis can be found at `http://www.imdb.com/title/tt0107048/synopsis`.

[8] A fuller discussion of these issues may be found in Levison and Lessard (2012).

5 Threads and threading of a DAG

A particular telling of a story, which we call here the *narrative*, may be conceived of as a particular traversal of the DAG. To designate this, we make use of the concept of *threading*. Threads are simply sequences of nodes and we often display them in the diagram of a DAG by a dotted line through the nodes. A thread need not follow the edges of the DAG, nor need it be acyclic. In other words, the same thread may traverse the same node more than once. The ordering of the threads of a narrative is assumed to correspond to narrative time. The various segments in our diagrams are numbered. Threads may traverse some but not necessarily all nodes of the DAG.

It should be noted that a particular DAG may give rise to numerous possible threadings. So, for example, a story may be told in chronological order ("Once upon a time, there was a beautiful princess ... she was kidnapped by an evil wizard ... a handsome prince rescued her ... they lived happily ever after."), or in reverse ("The prince and the princess were preparing for their wedding ... this was the outcome of his rescue of her ... she had been kidnapped..."). Furthermore, a DAG may be threaded to capture not just some telling of the narrative, but also in terms of the point of view of some character, the states of some object in the narrative, or the representation of space or description of places or characters.

We will apply this conceptual machinery to the analysis semantic repetition in the GH script.

6 Analysis

At an abstract level, the relationships behind GH (that is, the *story*) may be represented by three nodes joined by solid edges, which show the semantic dependencies among the nodes, as shown in Figure 1. The first sets the scene by placing Phil in Punxsutawney, the second represents Phil's recursive actions during his endless series of February 2's, and the third represents his escape from recursion.

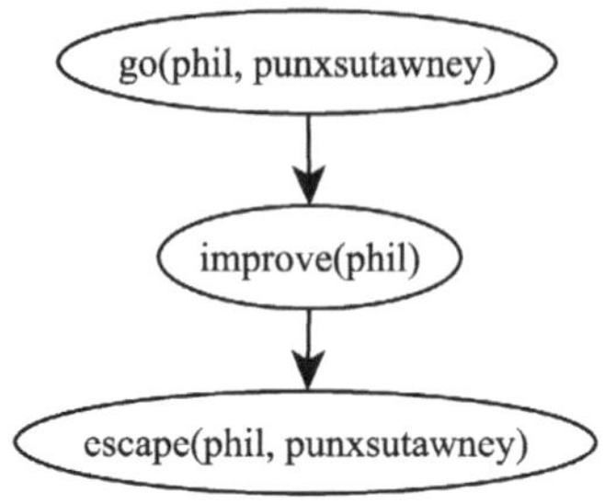

Figure 1: The most abstract DAG for GH

At the opposite extreme of granularity, it is possible to show the GH DAG with a thread traversing fine-grained nodes, each represented by a semantic expression. This representation, which contains 172 nodes and 171 edges, is far too large to fit onto a page. It may be viewed in its entirety at `http://tinyurl.com/awsb4x6`. As noted above, the segments of the thread are numbered and dotted. Following them in order thus recounts the semantic representation of the GH narrative at a relatively fine level of granularity. Between these two extremes of the abstract DAG and the linear threading, we will now examine several issues of semantic repetition.

6.1 Repetition as return of threads to a node

The simplest form of semantic repetition takes the form of a thread passing through some node more than once. Figure 2 provides a simple case of this.

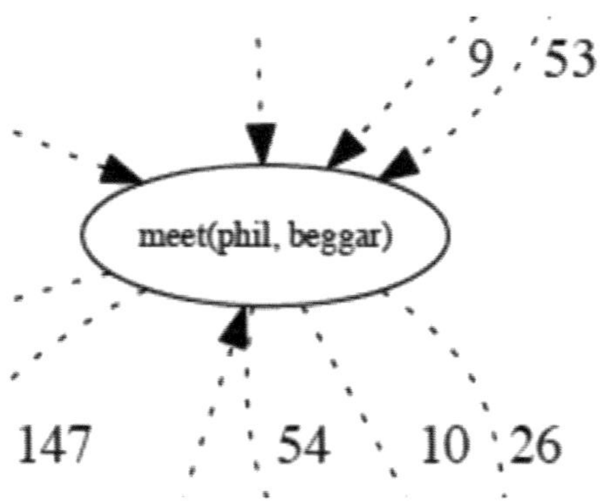

Figure 2: A thread passing multiple times through the same node

Thus, Phil meets a beggar at several points in the narrative (threads 9, 53, 146), with various outcomes, including ignoring the beggar (threads 10, 26, 54) and helping him (thread 147). Despite this help, the beggar dies (thread 148), but Phil is given the opportunity to replay this sequence (thread 149), choosing then to feed the beggar (thread 150).

6.2 DAGs and subDAGs

Consideration of the entire GH threading shows not just return of the thread to a single node, but also constellations of nodes which 'hang together'. In some cases, this is based on common membership of the nodes in some class of events. One example of this is provided by Phil's various attempts at suicide. Since Phil returns to life after each suicide, each suicide attempt (a toaster dropped into a bathtub, leaping from a tall building, walking in front of a bus, and so on) shares with the others only membership in the class of suicide events. This state of affairs may be captured by including each of these nodes within a local subDAG, which itself represents a subnode of the larger DAG. So, for example, we could represent the local subDAG here by means of the semantic expression `attempt(phil, suicide)`. Such subDAGs may be further refined or combined, similar to the concept of stepwise refinement found in computer programming.

In the case of the various suicide attempts, it is important to note that the various attempts show no dependency among themselves, and no order among them is required, beyond that imposed by a particular threading. This may be represented as follows:

```
kill(phil, phil, with(electricity))
kill(phil, phil, with(jump))
```

and so on. A similar example is found in Phil's attempts to improve himself, which involve learning Italian, music, sculpture and medicine, among other things.

However, we also find instances in which several nodes within a subDAG do show dependency relations within a common subDAG. So, for example, when Phil meets Rita at a bar, the same sequence is followed: he buys her a drink, they make a toast, and they discuss Rita's previous education, as can be seen in Figure 3.

Note that both temporal and logical dependence exists between two of the nodes (Phil must buy the drink in order for them to make a toast). There is no dependence between these two and the discussion of Rita's education, but the threading may indicate a temporal order.

Mixed models are also possible, in which some elements of a subDAG show dependency while others do not, as in the case where Phil awakens to the fact

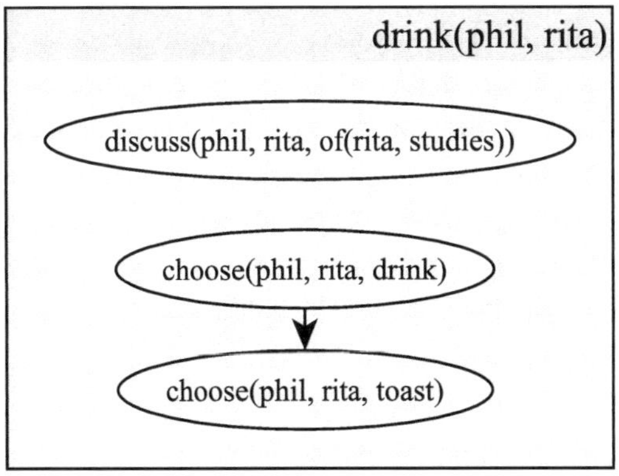

Figure 3: The subDAG for Phil and Rita at the bar

that his acts have no long-term consequences. In one reaction to this, he robs a bank, buys a car and tours the town. Each of these steps depends on the previous one. However, he also gets a tattoo and throws a party, both of which are independent of each other and of the others. However, together, all these elements constitute the subDAG of exploring the absence of consequences.

6.3 Parametrized subDAGs

In the presentation so far, we have treated the semantic expressions within nodes as constants. However, examination of the GH DAG brings to light several instances in which some part of the DAG is repeated with one or more elements replaced systematically with different ones. One illustration of this may be found in Phil's various reportings of the events at Gobbler's Knob, when the groundhog appears. Over the course of the narrative, he is first glib and sarcastic, then confused, then professional, then learned, poetic, and finally profound. This might be represented by five distinct copies of the part.

```
describe(phil, groundhog, ironic)
describe(phil, groundhog, confused)
```

and so on. However, given the similarity between the five nodes, it would be more efficient to create a single, separated, copy containing parameters, which could be instantiated in each of the five places with the parameters replaced by the appropriate variants.

A similar series of parameters may be found elsewhere in GH, for example, when Phil greets the man on the stairs of the B&B first ironically, then angrily, and finally with good humour, in Italian. Or again, at a more complex level, we find a series of instances where Phil learns some new skill (French poetry, piano, Italian, sculpture,...) and subsequently applies it. This is illustrated by two typical subDAGs in Figure 4.

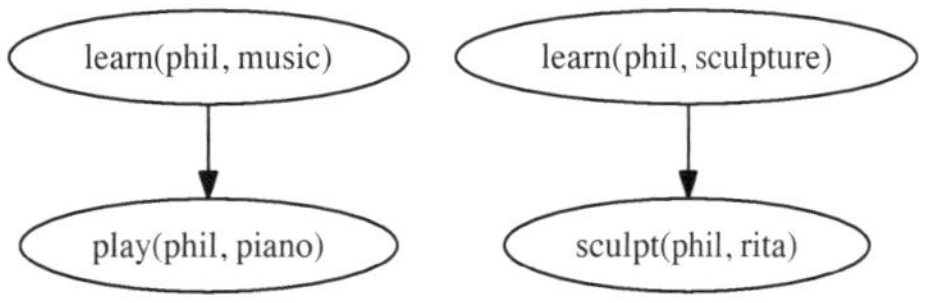

Figure 4: Learning and implementation

Each of these series forms a sequence such as:

```
improve(phil, altruism, 0)
improve(phil, altruism, 1)
```

and so on, where the third parameter indicates Phil's progression along the scale of character development. This particular series provides a means of capturing each particular state in Phil's evolution from egotist to altruist.

Note however that Phil's moral development does not progress through different areas of his life, one series at a time. In other words, he does not first change from a sarcastic to a poetic reporter, then grow from an egotist to an altruist in the community, then make the transformation from a seducer to an attentive lover, and so on. Rather, his personal improvement happens more or less at the same pace across different facets of his life, reflecting his overall personal growth, although evidence of this might be drawn first from one and then from another of his activities.

6.4 Parallel DAGs

In the discussion to this point, we have been concerned with repetition within a single subDAG. However, in GH, we also find instances where one subDAG shows an architectural similarity to another. This similarity can be construed as a sort of high-level repetition. For example, while on location in Punxsutawney, Phil meets and seduces Nancy, a woman from Punxsutawney. At the same time, he attempts to seduce Rita, his producer.

In both cases, Phil makes an initial attempt and is rebuffed, by both Nancy and Rita. Undaunted, he then seeks more information about both, determining Nancy's name and obtaining enough information to pass as a former high school classmate, and determining that Rita drinks tequila with lime, that she toasts world peace, and that she likes French poetry. He then uses the information about Nancy to seduce her, but the same tactic is unsuccessful with Rita.

The two parallel subDAGs may be represented by a higher-level subDAG where almost all the individual elements change from case to case, with only the general framework remaining. This might be expressed schematically as follows:

```
experiment(x,y) =
slist(
  meet(x,y)
  learn(x, of(y, characteristics)))
```

and so on.

Applied within a single narrative, such an approach deals with the sort of parallel cases seen here. Applied across narratives, it gives rise to texts seen as 'telling the same story', like *Romeo and Juliet* mentioned earlier. At an even more abstract level, it provides a means of modelling parodies, or works based on some previous model. Think of Joyce's *Ullysses*, in which Stephen Daedalus' peregrinations around Dublin represent a parellel to Homer's *Odyssey*.

6.5 Connections between subDAGs

We now have a means of representing semantic repetition at both the low level, of individual nodes of a DAG, as well as within and across DAGs. However, we have left unspecified an important point, to which we now return. Earlier, we showed that individual nodes may contain subDAGs of interior nodes, up to some indefinite level of complexity. This varying granularity provides a model for different degrees of detail in the recounting of a story, between the highest-level and coarsest summary, to the finest detail. Consider now the following case from GH. Each day, Phil wakes up, hears the same song on the radio, followed by inane banter from two disc jockeys. At the level of the DAG, this may be represented as an overarching node which contains two interior nodes, as shown formulaically here:

```
wakeup(phil) = slist(
  hear(phil, song)
  hear(phil, dj_banter))
```

and graphically in Figure 5.

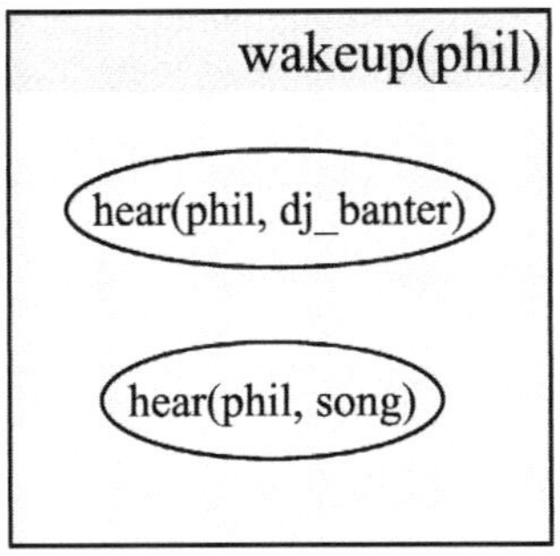

Figure 5: Part of the DAG for Phil's waking up

However, the actual threading of this higher-level nodes and its interior nodes in the narrative varies over the course of the narration, as shown in Figure 6.

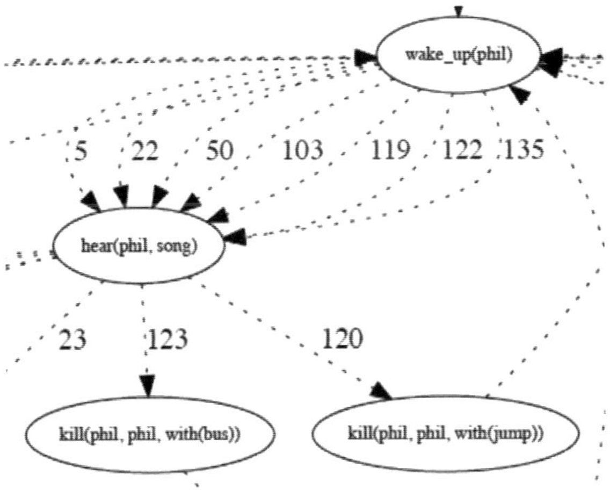

Figure 6: The threading of Phil's waking up

Thus, in threads 5, 22, 50, 103, 119, 122 and 135, Phil's waking up is followed by his hearing of the song, but in thread 36, Phil's waking up is followed immediately by the DJ banter. Similarly, threads 6, 23, 51 and 104 join the hearing of the song with the hearing of the banter, but in the case of threads 120 and 123, the recounting of Phil's hearing of the song is followed directly by suicide attempts, with no mention of the banter. In both these cases, we can presume that the DAG remains constant, but the threading represents either a complete traversal of all the interior nodes, or, typically later in the narrative, narrative 'shortcuts' which indicate the entire `wakeup` DAG by explicitly mentioning only some elements. Such shortcuts may be found in most narratives. For example, subsequent references to a known character or event may be reduced to the minimum, since a simple mention reactivates the entire reference. Conversely, the exploration of interior nodes rather than higher-level ones (in other words, providing more detail) may produce an effect of *slowdown* (Bal, 1985).

In the case of semantic repetition, shortcuts like those just described demonstrate that not only can repetition occur in the absence of repeated formal elements, but even in the absence of explicitly repeated semantic elements. At the extreme, the activation of a higher-level node by reference to an interior node provides a model for literary allusions, perhaps the most subtle type of repetition, where some element in one text activates a reference to another.

7 Conclusions and next steps

The series of examples presented here provide evidence for the existence of semantic repetition at both the atomic and structural levels. They also show that these can be captured by a model which permits various levels of granularity, from atomic semantic expressions to higher-level subDAGs and DAGs. It must be admitted however that, at this stage of the research, only human intelligence has permitted the identification of semantic repetition in its various forms. In an ideal world, a computer program might be capable of arriving at the same judgments. Work such as Chambers and Jurafsky (2008) or Hobbs et al. (1993) might provide a good starting point for this. In the meantime, we believe that there is value in continuing the *meaning-first* perspective illustrated here, as a complement to the more usual text-first analyses. When combined with a user-friendly formalism, this approach would go some way to bridging the divide between computer scientists and literary specialists in their analysis of literary texts.

References

Nicholas Asher and Alex Lascarides. 2003. *Logics of conversation*. Cambridge University Press, Cambridge.

Mieke Bal. 1985. *Narratology: introduction to the theory of narrative*. University of Toronto Press, Toronto.

Richard Bird. 1998. *Introduction to functional programming using Haskell*. Prentice-Hall, London, 2nd edition.

Charles Callaway and James Lester. 2001. Evaluating the effects of natural language generation techniques on reader satisfaction. In *Proceedings of the Twenty-Third Annual Conference of the Cognitive Science Society*, pages 164–169.

Charles Callaway and James Lester. 2002. Narrative prose generation. *Artificial Intelligence*, 139(2):213–252.

Nathanael Chambers and Dan Jurafsky. 2008. Unsupervised learning of narrative event chains. In *Proceedings of ACL-08: HLT*, pages 789–797.

Fiorella de Rosis and Floriana Grasso. 2000. Affective natural language generation. In A.M. Paiva, editor, *Affective instructions*, pages 204–218. Springer, Berlin.

Gérard Genette. 1972. *Figures III*. Editions du Seuil, Paris.

Gérard Genette. 1983. *Nouveau discours du récit*. Editions du Seuil, Paris.

Hermann Helbig. 2006. *Knowledge representation and the semantics of natural language*. Springer, Berlin.

Simon Hewitt. 2012. The logic of finite order. *Notre Dame Journal of Formal Logic*, 53(3):297–318.

Jerry R. Hobbs, Mark E. Stickel, Douglas E. Appelt, and Paul Martin. 1993. Interpretation as abduction. *Artificial Intelligence*, 63:69–142.

Roman Jakobson. 1960. Linguistics and poetics. In Thomas A Sebeok, editor, *Style in language*, pages 350–377. MIT, Cambridge, Mass.

Barbara Johnstone. 1991. *Repetition in Arabic discourse: paradigms, syntagms, and the ecology of language*. J. Benjamins, Amsterdam.

Greg Lessard, Stéfan Sinclair, Max Vernet, François Rouget, Elisabeth Zawisza, Louis-Émile Fromet de Rosnay, and Élise Blumet. 2004. Pour une recherche semi-automatisée des topoï narratifs. In P. Enjalbert and M. Gaio, editors, *Approches sémantiques du document électronique*, pages 113–130. Europia, Paris.

Michael Levison and Greg Lessard. 2012. Is this a DAG that I see before me? An onomasiological approach to narrative analysis and generation. In Mark Finlayson, editor, *The Third Workshop on Computational Models of Narrative*, pages 134–141, LREC Conference, Istanbul.

Michael Levison, Greg Lessard, Craig Thomas, and Matthew Donald. 2012. *The Semantic Representation of Natural Language*. Bloomsbury, London.

Inderjeet Mani. 2012. *Computational Modelling of Narrative*. Synthesis Lectures on Human Language Technologies. Morgan and Claypool.

William C. Mann and Sandra Thompson. 1988. Rhetorical Structure Theory: toward a functional theory of text organization. *Text*, 8(3):243–281.

Isidore Okpewho. 1992. *African oral literature: backgrounds, character, and continuity*. Indiana University Press, Bloomington.

Roger C. Schank and Robert P. Abelson. 1977. *Scripts, Plans, Goals and Understanding: An Inquiry into Human Knowledge Structures*. Lawerence Erlbaum Associates, Hillsdale, NJ.

Nicola Stanhope, Gillian Cohen, and Martin Conway. 1993. Very long-term retention of a novel. *Applied Cognitive Psychology*, 7:239–256.

Deborah Tannen. 1989. *Talking voices: repetition, dialogue, and imagery in conversational discourse*. Cambridge University Press, Cambridge.

Lucia M. Tovena and Marta Donazzan. 2008. On ways of repeating. *Recherches linguistiques de Vincennes*, 37:85–112.

Reuven Tsur. 2008. *Toward a theory of cognitive poetics*. Sussex Academic Press, Brighton, 2nd edition.

Exploring Cities in Crime: Significant Concordance and Co-occurrence in Quantitative Literary Analysis

Janneke Rauscher[1] **Leonard Swiezinski**[2] **Martin Riedl**[2] **Chris Biemann**[2]
(1) Johann Wolfgang Goethe University
Grüneburgplatz 1, 60323 Frankfurt am Main, Germany
(2) FG Language Technology, Dept. of Computer Science
Technische Universität Darmstadt, 64289 Darmstadt, Germany
j.rauscher@em.uni-frankfurt.de, floppy35@web.de,
{riedl,biem}@cs.tu-darmstadt.de

Abstract

We present CoocViewer, a graphical analysis tool for the purpose of quantitative literary analysis, and demonstrate its use on a corpus of crime novels. The tool displays words, their significant co-occurrences, and contains a new visualization for significant concordances. Contexts of words and co-occurrences can be displayed. After reviewing previous research and current challenges in the newly emerging field of quantitative literary research, we demonstrate how CoocViewer allows comparative research on literary corpora in a project-specific study, and how we can confirm or enhance our hypotheses through quantitative literary analysis.

1 Introduction

Recent years have seen a surge in Digital Humanities research. This area, touching on both the fields of computer science and the humanities, is concerned with making data from the humanities analysable by digitalisation. For this, computational tools such as search, visual analytics, text mining, statistics and natural language processing aid the humanities researcher. On the one hand, software permits processing a larger set of data in order to assess traditional research questions. On the other hand, this gives rise to a transformation of the way research is conducted in the humanities: the possibility of analyzing a much larger amount of data – yet in a quantitative fashion with all its necessary aggregation – opens the path to new research questions, and different methodologies for attaining them.

Although the number of research projects in Digital Humanities is increasing at fast pace, we still observe a gap between the traditional humanities scholars on the one side, and computer scientists on the other. While computer science excels in crunching numbers and providing automated processing for large amounts of data, it is hard for the computer scientist to imagine what research questions form the discourse in the humanities. In contrast to this, humanities scholars have a hard time imagining the possibilities and limitations of computer technology, how automatically generated results ought to be interpreted, and how to operationalize automatic processing in a way that its unavoidable imperfections are more than compensated by the sheer size of analysable material.

This paper resulted from a successful cooperation between a natural language processing (NLP) group and a literary researcher in the field of Digital Humanities. We present the CoocViewer analysis tool for literary and other corpora, which supports new angles in literary research through quantitative analysis.

In the Section 2, we describe the CoocViewer tool and review the landscape of previously available tools for our purpose. As a unique characteristic, CoocViewer contains a visualisation of significant concordances, which is especially useful for target terms of high frequency. In Section 3, we map the landscape of previous and current quantitative research in literary analysis, which is still an emerging and somewhat controversial sub-discipline. A use-case for the tool in the context of a specific project is laid out in Section 4, where a few examples illustrate how CoocViewer is used to confirm and generate hypotheses in literary analysis. Section 5 concludes and provides an outlook to further needs in tool support for quantative literary research.

2 CoocViewer - a Visual Corpus Browser

This section describes our CoocViewer visual corpus browsing tool. After shortly outlining necessary pre-processing steps, we illustrate and motivate the functionality of the graphical user interface. The tool was specifically designed to aid researchers from the humanities that do not have a background in computational linguistics.

2.1 Related Work

Whereas there exist a number of tools for visualizing co-occurrences, there is, to the best of our knowledge, no tool to visualize positional co-occurrences, or as we also call them, significant concordances. In (Widdows et al., 2002) tools are presented that visualize meanings of nouns as vector space representation, using LSA (Deerwester et al., 1990) and graph models using co-occurrences. There is also a range of text-based tools, without any quantitative statistics, e.g. Textpresso (Müller et al., 2004), PhraseNet[1] and Walden[2]. For searching words in context, Luhn (1960) introduced KWIC (Key Word in Context) which allows us to search for concordances and is also used in several corpus linguistic tools e.g. (Culy and Lyding, 2011), BNCWeb[3], Sketch Engine (Kilgarriff et al., 2004), Corpus Workbench[4] and MonoConc (Barlow, 1999). Although several tools for co-occurrences visualization exist (see e.g. co-occurrences for over 200 languages at LCC[5]), they often have different aims, and e.g. do not deliver the functionality to filter on different part-of-speech tags.

2.2 Corpus Preprocessing

To make a natural language corpus accessible in the tool, a number of preprocessing steps have to be carried out for producing the contents of CoocViewer's database. These steps consist of a fairly standard natural language processing pipeline, which we describe shortly.

After tokenizing, part-of-speech tagging (Schmid, 1994) and indexing the input data by document, sentence and paragraph within the document, we compute signficant sentence-wide and paragraph-wide co-occurrences, using the tinyCC[6] tool. Here, the log-likelihood test (Dunning, 1993) is employed to determine the significance $sig(A, B)$ of the co-occurrence of two tokens A and B. To support the significant concordance view (described in the next section), we have extended the tool to also produce *positional* significant co-occurrences, where $sig(A, B, offset)$ is computed by the log-likelihood significance of the co-occurrence of A and B in a token-distance of $offset$. Since the significance measure requires the single frequencies of A and B, as well as their joint frequency *per positional offset* in this setup, this adds considerable overhead during preprocessing. To our knowledge, we are the first to extend the notion of positional co-occurrence beyond direct neighbors, cf. (Richter et al., 2006). We apply a sigificance threshold of 3.84[7] and a frequency threshold of 2 to only keep 'interesting' pairs. The outcome of preprocessing is stored in a MySQL database schema similar to the one used by LCC (Biemann et al., 2007). We store sentence- and paragraph-wide co-occurrences and positional co-occurrences in separate database tables, and use one database per corpus. The database tables are indexed accordingly to optimize the queries issued by the CoocViewer tool. Additionally, we map the part-of-speeches to E (proper names), N (proper nouns), A (adjectives), V (verbs), R (all other part-of-speech tags) for an uniform representation for different languages.

2.3 Graphical User Interface

The graphical user interface (UI) is built with common web technologies, such as HTML, CSS and JavaScript. The UI communicates via AJAX with a backend, which utilizes PHP and a MySQL

[1] http://www-958.ibm.com/software/data/cognos/manyeyes/page/Phrase_Net.html

[2] http://infomotions.com/sandbox/network-diagrams/bin/walden/

[3] http://bncweb.lancs.ac.uk/bncwebSignup/user/login.php

[4] http://cwb.sourceforge.net

[5] http://corpora.uni-leipzig.de/

[6] http://wortschatz.uni-leipzig.de/~cbiemann/software/TinyCC2.html, (Richter et al., 2006)

[7] corresponding to 5% error probability

database. This makes the approach flexible regarding the platform. It can run on client computers using XAMP[8], a portable package of various Web technologies, including an Apache web server and a MySQL server. Alternatively, the tool can operate as a client-server application over a network. In particular, we want to highlight the JavaScript data visualization framework D3 (Bostock et al., 2011), which was used to layout and draw the graphs. We deliberately designed the tool to match the requirements of literary researchers, who are at times overwhelmed by general-purpose visualisation tools such as e.g. Gephi[9]. The UI is split into three parts: At the top a menu bar, including a search input field and search options, a graph drawing panel and display options at the bottom of the page.

Figure 1: Screenshot of the Coocviewer application using the concordance view.

The menu bar allows switching between co-occurrence and concordance views (see Figure 1). The search field supports wildcards and type-ahead autocompletion, immediately displaying which words exist in the corpus and match the current input. Additionally, there are functionalities to export the shown graph as SVG or PNG image, or as plain text, containing all relations, including their frequencies and significance scores. Within the advanced configuration windows (shown on the right side) one can select different corpora, enable case sensitive/insensitive searches or filter words according their part-of-speech tags (as described in Section 2.2). The graph drawing panel visualizes the queried term and its significant co-occurrences resp. concordances, significancy being visualized by the thickness of the lines. In Figure 1, showing the concordances for *bread*, we can directly see words that occur often with *bread* in the context: E.g. *bread* is often used in combination with *butter, cheese, margarine* (offset +2), but also the kind of different breads is described by the adjectives at offset -1. For the same information, using the normal KWIC view, one has to count the words with different offset by hand to find properties for the term *bread*. At the bottom, the maximal number of words shown in the graph can be specified. For the concordances display there is an additional option to specify the maximal offset. The original text (with provenance information) containing the nodes (words) or edges (word pairs) shown in the graph can be retrieved by either clicking on a word itself or on the edge connecting two words, in a new window (see Figure 2) within the application. This window also provides informa-

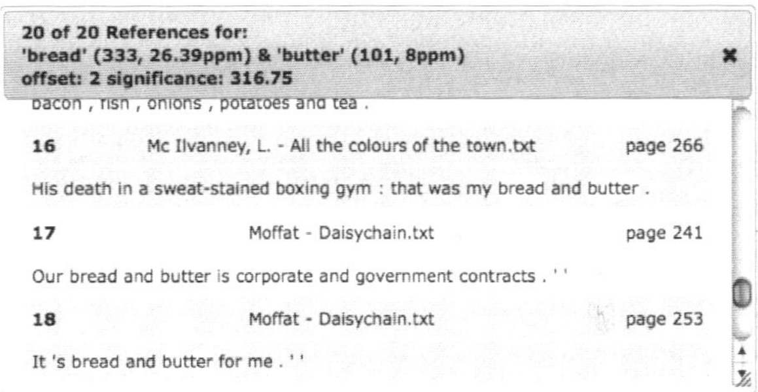

Figure 2: Occurrences of a significant concordance

tion about the frequencies of single words as well as their co-occurrence, and also displays relative single word frequencies in parts-per-million (ppm) to enable comparisons between corpora of different sizes. Words in focus are highlighted and the contents of this window can also be exported as plain text.

3 Quantitative Literary Research

Quantitative research in literary analysis, although being conducted and discussed since at least the 1960s, (Hoover, 2008), is still far from being a clear field of research with a verified and acknowledged methodology. Studies in this field vary widely with respect to scope, methods applied and theoretical

[8] http://www.apachefriends.org/en/index.html

[9] https://gephi.org/

background. Until now, only the most basic definition can be given that applies to these approaches: Quantitative research in literary analysis is generally concerned with the application of methods from corpus linguistics (and statistics) to the field of literature to investigate and quantify general grammatical and lexical features of texts.

Most studies applying such methods to literary analysis are carried out in the field of stylistics, building a relatively new research area of corpus stylistics, also called stylometry (Mahlberg, 2007; Hoover, 2008; Biber, 2011). The quantitative exploration of stylistic features and patterns is used for authorship attribution, e.g. (Burrows, 1992; Burrows, 2007; Craig, 2004; Hoover, 2001; Hoover, 2002), exploring the specificity of one author's style, e.g. (Burrows, 1987; Hori, 2004; Fischer-Starcke, 2010; Mahlberg, 2012) or one certain text, often compared to other texts of the same author or period, e.g. (Craig, 1999; McKenna and Antonia, 2001; Stubbs, 2005; Clement, 2008; Fischer-Starcke, 2009). Some studies focus on content-related questions such as the analysis of plot or characterization and the exploration of relations between and role of different characters, e.g. (Mahlberg, 2007; Culpeper, 2002; Culpeper, 2009), developing new ways of exploring these literary features, e.g. via the application of social network analysis (Elson et al., 2010; Moretti, 2011; Agarwal et al., 2012). Besides this area, there are numerous other approaches, like the attempt to investigate the phenomenon of "literary creativity" (Hoey, 2007) or ways for automatic recognition of literary genres (Allison et al., 2011).

Major methodological approaches of this field are, according to Biber (2011), Mahlberg (2007) and Hoover (2008), the study of keywords and word-frequencies, co-occurrences, lexical clusters (also called bundles or n-grams) and collocational as well as concordance analysis. Additionally, the need for cross-investigating and comparing the results with other corpora (be it a general corpus of one language or other small, purpose-built corpora) is emphasized to discuss the uniqueness of the results.

But while especially the studies of Moretti (2000; 2007; 2009), taking a quantitative approach of "distant reading" on questions of literary history and the evolution of literary genres, are often received as groundbreaking for the case, and despite the rising interest in this field of research in the last decades, there still is much reluctance towards the implementation of such methods. The general arguments raised frequently from the point of view of 'classical' literary analysis against a quantitative or computational approach can be grouped around four central points: The uniqueness of each literary text that quantitative analysis seems to underscore when treating the texts just as examples of style or period, focussing on very general patterns; the emphasize of technology and the relatively high threshold that the application, analysis and interpretation of the generated data contains (Potter, 1988); and the general notion that meaning in literary texts is highly context-related and context-dependent in different ways (Hoover, 2008). Last but not least there is what can be called the "so-what-argument": Quantitative methods tend to produce sparse significant new information compared with the classical approach of close reading, generating insights and interpretations that could as well be reached by simply reading the book (Mahlberg, 2007; Rommel, 2008). But the possibilities and advantages of corpus linguistics come to the foreground especially if one is not interested in aspects of uniqueness or particularity but in commonalities and differences between large amounts of literary texts too many to be read and compared in the classical way. This especially holds when it comes to questions of topics, themes, discourse analysis and the semantisation of certain words.

4 Empirical Analysis

This section describes a few exemplary analysis which we carried out within our ongoing project "At the crime scene: The intrinsic logic of cities in contemporary crime novels". Settled between the disciplines of sociology and literature, the project is embedded in the urban sociological research area of the 'Eigenlogik' (intrinsic logic) of cities (Berking, 2012; Löw, 2012; Löw, forthcoming). The basic hypothesis is that there is no such thing as 'the' city or 'the' urban experience in general, but that every city forms its own contexts and complexes of meaning, the unquestioned and often subconsciously operating knowledge of how things are done, respectively making sense of the city. To put it another way, we want to find out if and in what way the respective city makes a difference and is forming distinctive structures of thought, action and feeling. This is explored simultaneously in four different projects investigating different fields (economic practices, city marketing, problem discourses and literary field and texts) in four different cities that are compared with each other (Birmingham (UK), Glasgow, Frankfurt on the Main and Dortmund). If the hypothesis is right, the four different investigated fields should have more in common within one city and across the fields than within one field across different cities.

Our subproject is mainly concerned with the literary and cultural imagination and representation of the cities in question. One crucial challenge is the exploration, analysis and comparison of 240 contemporary crime novels, each of them set in one of the cities under examination. The aim of this explorative study is to analyze the possibility and characteristics of city-specific structures within the realm of literary representations of cities.

Dealing with such comparably large amounts of literary texts, a tool was needed that facilitated us (laypeople in the field of corpus linguistics) to explore the city-specific content and structures within these corpora, enabling a connection of qualitative close reading and quantitative methods. Visualization was a major concern, apparently lowering the resistance of the literary research community towards charts and numbers and making the results readable and interpretable without having much expertise in corpus linguistics. Moreover, the option of generating significant concordances instead of simple concordance lines (as e.g. with KWIC) is very promising: Confronted with very high word frequencies for some of our search terms, e.g. more than 2200 occurrences of "Frankfurt" in our Frankfurt corpus, completely manual analysis turned out to be painstaking and very time-consuming. Automated or manual reduction of the number of lines according to standard practices, as e.g. suggested by Tribble (2010), is not possible without potential loss of information. CoocViewer enables a sophisticated and automated analysis with concentration on statistically significant findings through clustering co-occurring words according to their statistical significance in concordance lines. Additionally, the positionality of these re-occurring co-occurrences in relation to the search term (with a maximum range from -10 to +10 around the node) gives a clear and immediate picture of patterns of usage within a corpus. Via exploring the references of the results we are still able to take account of the context-specificity of literary texts, as well as distinguishing author-specific results from those distributed more equally across a corpus.

City	lang.	#novels	#tokens	#sent.	#para.
Birmingham	engl.	41	4.8M	336K	142K
Glasgow	engl.	61	7.7M	496K	222K
Dortmund	ger.	59	5.0M	361K	127K
Frankfurt	ger.	79	8.0M	546K	230K

Table 1: Quantitative characteristics of our corpora

After describing the corpus resources, we conduct two exemplary analysis to show how the quantitative tool as described in Section 2 can be used to aid complex qualitative research interests in the humanities through supporting the exploration and comparison of large corpora (Sect. 4.2), as well as investigating and comparing the semantization and semantic preference of words (Sect. 4.3). The discussion of results shows how CoocViewer can support hypothesis building and testing on a quantitative basis, linking qualitative and quantitative approaches.

4.1 Corpus

The selection of the crime novels was based on three criteria: contemporariness (written and published within the past 30 years until 2010), the city in question (should play a major role resp. be used as major setting), and genre (crime fiction in any variety). In a first step, the 240 novels (gathered as paperback-editions) had to be scanned and digitalized[10]. Metadata was removed and the remaining texts were preprocessed as described in Section 2.2. The novels were compiled in different corpora according to the city they are set in, and the database underlying them (sentence or paragraph). Table 1 provides an overview of the quantitative characteristics of the four city-specific corpora we discuss here.

[10]We used ABBY FineReader 10 professional for optical character recognition, which generated tolerable but not perfect results, making extensive proof reading and corrections necessary.

4.2 Analysis 1: Exploring the Use of the City's Name

The occurrence of the name of a city in crime novels can serve different purposes and functions in the text. It can be used, for example, to simply 'place' the plot (instead of or additionally to describing the setting in further detail) or to indicate the direction of movement of figures ("they drove to Glasgow"). Often it is surrounded by information about city-specific aspects, e.g. of history or materiality. Searching for the respective proper names of the cities in the four corpora therefore seems to be a promising start to explore the possibility of city-specific structures of meaning in literary representation. If the 'Eigenlogik'-hypothesis is right, not only the content that is associated with the name (what would generally be expected) but also its frequent usages and functions (as pointer or marker, as starting point for further explanations of city life, etc.) should differ systematically across cities.

A first close reading of some exemplary crime novels already suggested that this could be the case. To check this qualitatively derrived impression we conducted CoocViewer searches for the top-15 significant co-occurrences across all parts of speech for each proper name in the respective corpus on sentence level (see Figure 3 for the cases of Glasgow and Frankfurt). To interpret and compare these findings, we additionally looked at the significant concordances (with the same search parameters and an offset from the node of -3/+3), which helps to analyze and refine the findings in more depth. In the following, we discuss, compare and interpret the results with respect to our overriding project-hypothesis to verify or falsify some of our qualitative first impressions quantitatively.

The corpora indeed tend not only to vary significantly with respect to the sheer frequency of the usage of the proper name (with relative frequencies ranging from Glasgow (324ppm) and Frankfurt (286ppm) to Dortmund (187ppm) and Birmingham (154ppm)), but also in the usages and functions that the naming fulfills. The graphs reveal not only differing co-occurrences, but also differing proportions of co-occurring word classes, each city revealing its own distinct pattern.

Especially the English cities tend to co-occur with

Figure 3: Significant co-occurrences of "Glasgow" (upper) and "Frankfurt" (lower) in their respective corpora

proper names and common nouns (ten proper names, four common nouns in the case for Glasgow, eight names and six nouns for Birmingham).[11] For Glasgow, these comprise parts of the inventory of the city (with "City" (sig. of 695.57) as either part of the name or city-specific institution ("City of Glasgow", "City Orchestra") or to refer to different crime-genre specific institutions (as the "City of Glasgow Police" or "Glasgow City Mortuary")), the "University" (sig. of 380.42), or the park "Glasgow Green" (233.46). There is also the name of another city, the Scottish capital (and rival city) Edinburgh. As the statistical concordances reveal quickly, the "Port" (350.88) is, despite Glasgow's history as shipbuilding capital, not used to refer to the cities industrial past. Instead, as can bee seen from its positioning on -1 directly left to the node, it refers to the small nearby town Port Glasgow (see

[11] The noun "accent" which both English cities names co-occur with (and for which no equivalent term can be found on the German side) can be explained by a different lexicalization of the concept, which is realized through derivation in German.

Fig. 4). The co-occurrence of "Royal" and Glasgow (being not a royal city) can also be easily explained via the concordance view, showing that this is mainly due to the "Royal Concert Hall" (forming a strong triangle on positions +1, +2 and +3 from the node). Besides these instances of places and institutions within and around the city, especially the connection to the pronoun "its" (82 instances with a sig. of 144) is interesting. None of the other cities shows a top-significant co-occurrence with a comparable pronoun. A look at the corresponding references in the corpus shows that it is mainly used in statements about the quality or speciality of certain aspects of the city (indicated on graphic level through the connections between "its" and "city" or "area") and in personifications (e.g. "Glasgow could still reach out with its persistent demands"). This implies that the literary device of anthropomorphization of the city (in direct connection with the proper name) occurs more often within Glasgow-novels than within those of the other cities, and that there are many explicit statements about "how this city (or a special part of it) is", showing a tendency to explain the city. Furthermore, the exploration of the different references indicates a relatively 'coherent corpus' (and, therefore, relatively stable representation) with recurring instances across many authors.

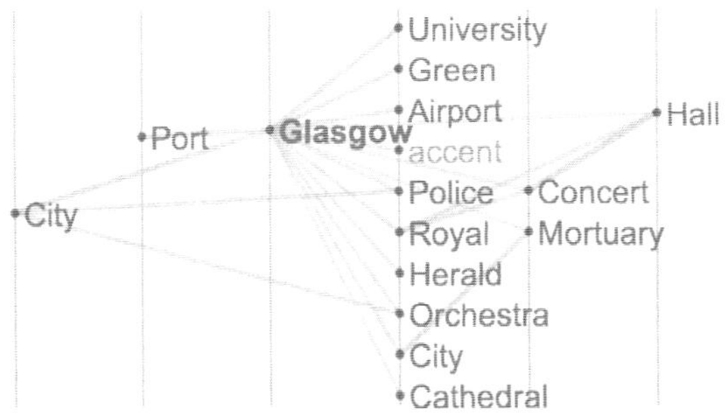

Figure 4: Significant concordances of "Glasgow" in Glasgow corpus

In contrast to this, Birmingham's co-occurring proper names mainly refer to (fictive) names of newspapers (the Birmingham "Sentinel", "Post" and "News"). The inventory of the city is not very prominently represented, with "University" (sig. of 152.52) and "Airport" (80.63) as the only instances. Furthermore, the University tends to be represented as region-, not city-specific (with a stronger connection between "University" and "Midlands" (sig. of 200.49) than between both words to the city itself ("Midlands" co-occurring with a sig. of 68.68)). The rest of the proper names relates to not further specified parts of the city ("East" (71.62) and "North-East" (73.43)). The word "south" appears as adverb, reflecting on graphic level that it is more often used as in "heading south" than referring to the "south of Birmingham". Also, the noun "city" (sig. of 154.53) is often related to the "city centre" (indicated through the very strong link between those two words), but also to make statements like "Birmingham is a city that" or "like other cities, Birmingham has". The references reveal the quality of this explanations, rather stressing its ordinariness as city instead of personalizing it or emphasizing its uniqueness. This indicates that the city itself is not standing prominently in the foreground in its crime novels (in contrast to Glasgow and in accordance with our qualitatively derived prior results). The proper name is mainly used as part of other proper names (e.g. "Birmingham Sentinel"), fulfilling the function of simply placing the plot, and there is very little city-specific information given on a statistical significant re-occurring level in the closer surroundings of it. Even the statements about Birmingham as a city tend to downplay its singularity.

On the German side, the cities names co-occur with words from a wider range of word classes. For both cities, we find less co-occurring proper names: five for Frankfurt, only one of them referring to a city-specific aspect (the long version of the name "Frankfurt on the Main" (sig. of 585.09)); four for Dortmund (again, only one city-specific, the name of its soccer club "Borussia" (with only seven instances and a sig. of 41.93)). For both cities, the rest of the proper names is composed of names of other cities (in Frankfurt the two nearby cities "Offenbach" (139.49) and "Darmstadt" (105.73), and "Berlin", "Hamburg"); for Dortmund only cities from the same metropolitan area (the Ruhrgebiet), "Düsseldorf" (41.95), "Werne" (41.78) and "Duisburg" (39.42)). It seems that Dortmund is closely connected within the metropolitan area it is a part of, but looking at the references shows that only Düsseldorf plays a role across different crime novel series, while the rest mainly feature in one certain series (being rated as author-specifc).

In the case of Frankfurt, the nouns that co-occur (seven) either denote city-specific aspects (Flughafen (airport) (96.83) and Eintracht (the local soccer club with a sig. of 192.36)) or very general instances (December, Jahren (years)). A look at the statistical concordances, ordered according not only to their position around the node but also to their significance, displays that the noun "Kripo" (short form for crime investigation unit) on the -1 position is more often used than the first city-specific instance, with a significance of 564.58 (while "police" for Glasgow on the +1 position is relatively ranked lower). This prominent position of the crime investigation unit (interpreted as impact of genre-related aspects) indicates that there are many "police-procedural" crime novels in Frankfurt (which is true), giving insight into the sub-genre composition of the corpus. As with the English cities, the word "Stadt" (city; sig. of 245.63) co-occurs frequently, and as the references reveal it serves similar purposes: either to denote the political administration (the "Stadt Frankfurt") or in combination with further explanations of "how this city is" (as in Glasgow, but without personalization), or "Frankfurt is a city that", but in contrast to Birmingham not with a frequent downplaying of uniqueness. Additionally, we find instances where other cities are compared to Frankfurt ("a city that, unlike/like Frankfurt"). This seems to point towards a more flexible use of this combination resp. to a variety of ways of representation. Frankfurt is represented as a city allowing for different semantizations and different ways of depicting it without posing contradictions (as the differing uses occur not only across a wide range of authors, but within the same texts).
Finally, taking a closer look at Dortmund, the frequently co-occurring nouns nearly all are related to genre-specific instances, referring to crime investigation-related institutions (again "Kripo" (sig. of 88.91); "Polizeipräsidium" (police headquarters; sig. of 35.15), "Landgericht" (district court; 37.25) and "Sonderstaatsanwaltschaft" (34.63)). This indicates that in this corpus the genre-specific structures seem to imprint themselves more than the city-specific ones, putting the city itself into the background (similar to the case of Birmingham but with a highly differing pattern). But we also have to consider the comparably low relative frequency rates (ppm) that demand an explanation. There might be another similarity between Dortmund and Birmingham, both showing low relative frequencies for their respective proper names. But as we take a closer look on the references of the occurrences of the names, we can see that the one series of crime novels that represents the biggest share of the corpus (with 21 novels belonging to this series) does not mention "Dortmund" at all, while for Birmingham the use of the proper name is quite equally distributed across all authors and series. A look inside one of this books of the series in question reveals a possible answer to the low frequencies: instead of using the proper name, the author consequently uses the nickname "Bierstadt" (Beer-city). Therefore, while it is possible to show that each city under investigation reveals a specific pattern of co-occurrences and differing uses and functions of its proper name, as our hypothesis has suggested, the search for the proper name alone seems not sufficient to get the overall picture of the literary representation of a city, demanding further analysis.

4.3 Analysis 2: Investigating Genre Aspects

When it comes to questions of genre-conventions vs. city-conventions, the investigation of the semantic preference of typically crime-related words is interesting. If the specific city has an impact on genre-aspects, the graphs should show clear differences. Close reading of exemplary novels of Glasgow and Birmingham indicated that violence plays a greater role in Glasgow crime fiction than in that of Birmingham, therefore we expect to find differing attributions towards and meanings of "violence", showing a higher vocabulary richness in Glasgow than in Birmingham, taking into account its semantic preference (for more details about this aspect see e.g. (Hoey, 2007)). We examine this hypothesis through making "violence" the node of a search for significant concordances, searching for the top-30 adjectives directly altering the noun within a range of -3 to +3 around the node.

As depicted in Figure 5, our initial hypothesis can be verified. While Glasgow (upper) has nine significantly co-occurring adjectives (six directly altering the noun "violence" on pos. -1), Birmingham (lower) only has five (four on pos. -1). Those that directly alter the noun show a slightly differing seman-

Figure 5: Significant adjective concordances of "violence", comparing Glasgow (upper) and Birmingham (lower) corpora

tic preference, with adjectives of "kind of violence" (domestic, physical) standing on top in both corpora. Next, we look at adjectives that bear a notion of "quality or intensity of violence": while Birmingham only discriminates between mindless and latent violence, the vocabulary of Glasgow is much richer (thuggish, mindless, sudden), one of them also bearing a notion of expectability (sudden). Additionally, a temporal adjective is used to refer to "past violence". If we look at the instances on the -3 position for Glasgow (a position that is not filled for Birmingham), we can add random to the list of "quality of violence", and find some instances of "being afraid of (physical) violence" (as the link between those words implies). This verifies our close reading interpretations.

The adjectives to the right of the node ("own" on position +3 in Glasgow, "old" on position +2 in Birmingham) pose a puzzle. Through a look at the references for this instances, we can see that in the case of Birmingham, old is referring to victims of violence (old people), while the picture for Glasgow is split between violence of its own type (which then could be added to the list of quality-adjectives) and violence that one experienced on his own. Through the interconnectedness of the adjectives settled on different positions for the case of Glasgow and a look at the resources of the instances, we conclude that the patterns seem to be more established on city level (showing instances from varying authors for all adjective-noun combinations) than they are in Birmingham, where there are no cross-connections and the authors differ more among each other (with "physical violence" being the only combination that occurs across different authors, while all other adjective-noun combinations only appear within the work of a single author).

5 Conclusion and Further Work

To conclude the exemplary analysis, CoocViewer helps not only to explore large corpora but also to verify or relativize impressions from classical qualitative literary research. It opens up new ways of exploring topics, themes and relationships within large sets of literary texts. Especially the combination and linkage of co-occurrences and significant concordances simplifies the analysis and allows a finer-grained and more focused analysis than KWIC concordances or simple frequency counts. The possibility to distinguish between these two viewpoints on the data accelerates and improves the interpretation of results. Additionally, the comparison between corpora is much facilitated through the immediate visibility of differing patterns. Further work can proceed along a few lines. We would like to enable investigations of the wide context of co-occurrences through access from the references back to the whole crime-novel document. Further, we would like to automatically compare corpora of the same language on the level of local co-occurrence and concordance graphs to aid generating hypotheses. This will make a change in the interface necessary to support a comparative view. Furthermore, we want to extend the view of the original text (see Figure 2) in our tool by centering the sentences according to the selected word or words, as done in KWIC views. When clicking on a single word, this would lead to the normal KWIC view, but selecting an edge we then want to center the sentences according to the two words connected by the edge, which might be useful especially for the concordances.

The tool and the pre-processing software is available as an open source project[12] and as a web demo.

Acknowledgments

This work has been funded by the Hessian research excellence program *Landes-Offensive zur Entwicklung Wissenschaftlich-Ökonomischer Exzellenz (LOEWE)* as part of the research center *Digital Humanities*.

[12] `https://sourceforge.net/p/coocviewer`

References

Apoorv Agarwal, Augusto Corvalan, Jacob Jensen, and Owen Rambow. 2012. Social network analysis of alice in wonderland. In *Workshop on Computational Linguistics for Literature*, pages 88–96, Montréal, Canada.

Sahra Allison, Ryan Heuser, Mathhew Jockers, Franco Moretti, and Michael Witmore. 2011. *Quantitative Formalism: an Experiment*. Stanford Literary Lab.

M. Barlow. 1999. Monoconc 1.5 and paraconc. *International journal of corpus linguistics*, 4(1):173–184.

Helmuth Berking. 2012. The distinctiveness of cities: outline of a research programme. *Urban Research & Practice*, 5(3):316–324.

Douglas Biber. 2011. Corpus linguistics and the study of literature. back to the future? *Scientific Study of Literature*, 1(1):15–23.

Chris Biemann, Gerhard Heyer, Uwe Quasthoff, and Matthias Richter. 2007. The Leipzig Corpora Collection - monolingual corpora of standard size. In *Proceedings of Corpus Linguistics 2007*, Birmingham, UK.

Michael Bostock, Vadim Ogievetsky, and Jeffrey Heer. 2011. D3: Data-driven documents. *IEEE Trans. Visualization & Comp. Graphics (Proc. InfoVis)*.

John F. Burrows. 1987. *Computation into Criticism. A Study of Jane Austen's Novels and an Experiment in Method*. Clarendon, Oxford.

John F. Burrows. 1992. Computers and the study of literature. In Christopher S. Butler, editor, *Computers and Written Texts*, pages 167–204, Oxford. Blackwell.

John F. Burrows. 2007. All the way through: Testing for authorship in different frequency strata. *Literary and Linguistic Computing*, 22(1):27–47.

Tanya E. Clement. 2008. 'A thing not beginning and not ending': using digital tools to distand-read Gertrude Stein's The Making of Americans. *Literary and Linguistic Computing*, 23(3):361–381.

Hugh Craig. 1999. Jonsonian chronology and the styles of a tale of a tub. In Martin Butler, editor, *Re-Presenting Ben Jonson: Text, History, Performance*, pages 210–232, Houndmills. Macmillan.

Hugh Craig. 2004. Stylistic analysis and authorship studies. In Susan Schreibman, Ray Siemens, and John Unsworth, editors, *A Companion to Digital Humanities*. Blackwell.

Jonathan Culpeper. 2002. Computers, language and characterisation: An analysis of six characters in Romeo and Juliet. In Ulla Melander-Marttala, Carin Ostman, and Merja Kyt, editors, *Conversation in Life and Literature: Papers from the ASLA Symposium*, volume 15, pages 11–30, Uppsala. Association Suedoise de Linguistique Appliquee.

Jonathan Culpeper. 2009. Keyness: Words, parts-of-speech and semantic categories in the character-talk of shakespeare's romeo and juliet. *International Journal of Corpus Linguistics*, 14(1):29–59.

Chris Culy and Verena Lyding. 2011. Corpus clouds - facilitating text analysis by means of visualizations. In Zygmunt Vetulani, editor, *Human Language Technology. Challenges for Computer Science and Linguistics*, volume 6562 of *Lecture Notes in Computer Science*, pages 351–360. Springer Berlin Heidelberg.

Scott Deerwester, Susan T. Dumais, George W. Furnas, Thomas K. Landauer, and Richard Harshman. 1990. Indexing by latent semantic analysis. *Journal of the American Society for Information Science*, 41:391–407.

Ted Dunning. 1993. Accurate methods for the statistics of surprise and coincidence. *Computational Linguistics*, 19(1):61–74, March.

David K. Elson, Nicholas Dames, and Kathleen R. McKeown. 2010. Extracting social networks from literary fiction. In *48th Annual Meeting of the Association for Computer Linguistics*, pages 138–147, Uppsala, Sweden.

Bettina Fischer-Starcke. 2009. Keywords and frequent phrases of Jane Austen's Pride and Prejudice: A corpus-stylistc analysis. *International Journal of Corpus Linguistics*, 14(4):492–523.

Bettina Fischer-Starcke. 2010. *Corpus linguistics in literary analysis: Jane Austen and her contemporaries*. Continuum, London.

Carsten Görg, Hannah Tipney, Karin Verspoor, Jr. Baumgartner, William A., K. Bretonnel Cohen, John Stasko, and Lawrence E. Hunter. 2010. Visualization and language processing for supporting analysis across the biomedical literature. In *Knowledge-Based and Intelligent Information and Engineering Systems*, volume 6279 of *Lecture Notes in Computer Science*, pages 420–429. Springer Berlin Heidelberg.

Michael Hoey. 2007. Lexical priming and literary creativity. In Michael Hoey, Michaela Mahlberg, Michael Stubbs, and Wolfgang Teubert, editors, *Text, Discourse and Corpora. Theory and Analysis*, pages 31–56, London. Continuum.

David L. Hoover. 2001. Statistical stylistics and authorship attribution: an emprirical investigation. *Literary and Linguistic Computing*, 16(4):421–444.

David L. Hoover. 2002. Frequent word sequences and statistical stylistics. *Literary and Linguistic Computing*, 17(2):157–180.

David L. Hoover. 2008. Quantitative analysis and literary studies. In Ray Siemens and Susan Schreibman, editors, *A Companion to Digital Literary Studies*, Oxford. Blackwell.

Masahiro Hori. 2004. *Investigating Dicken's Style: A Collocational Analysis*. Palgrave Macmillan, Basingstoke.

Adam Kilgarriff, Pavel Rychly, Pavel Smrz, and David Tugwell. 2004. The sketch engine. In *Proceedings of EURALEX*, pages 105–116, Lorient, France.

Martina Löw. 2012. The intrinsic logic of cities: towards a new theory on urbanism. *Urban Research & Practice*, 5(3):303–315.

Martina Löw. forthcoming. The city as experential space: The production of shared meaning. *International Journal of Urban and Regional Research*.

H. P. Luhn. 1960. Key word-in-context index for technical literature (KWIC index). *American Documentation*, 11(4):288–295.

Michaela Mahlberg. 2007. Corpus stylistics: bridging the gap between linguistic and literary studies. In Michael Hoey, Michaela Mahlberg, Michael Stubbs, and Wolfgang Teubert, editors, *Text, Discourse and Corpora. Theory and Analysis*, pages 217–246, London. Continuum.

Michaela Mahlberg. 2012. *Corpus Stylistics and Dicken's Fiction*. Routledge advances in corpus linguistics. Routledge, London.

C. W. F. McKenna and Alexis Antonia. 2001. The statistical analysis of style: Reflections on fom, meaning, and ideology in the 'Nausicaa' episode of Ulysses. *Literary and Linguistic Computing*, 16(4):353–373.

Franco Moretti. 2000. Conjectures on world literature. *New Left Review*, 1(January/February):54–68.

Franco Moretti. 2007. *Graphs, Maps, Trees. Abstract Models for Literary History*. Verso, London / New York.

Franco Moretti. 2009. Style, Inc. reflections on seven thousand titels (British novels, 1740-1850). *Critical Inquiry*, 36(1):134–158.

Franco Moretti. 2011. *Network Theory, Plot Analysis*. Stanford Literary Lab.

Hans-Michael Müller, Eimear E. Kenny, and Paul W. Sternberg. 2004. Textpresso: An ontology-based information retrieval and extraction system for biological literature. *Plos Biology*, 2(11).

Rosanne G. Potter. 1988. Literary criticism and literary computing: The difficulties of a synthesis. *Computers and Humanities*, 22:91–97.

Matthias Richter, Uwe Quasthoff, Erla Hallsteinsdóttir, and Chris Biemann. 2006. Exploiting the Leipzig Corpora Collection. In *Proceesings of the IS-LTC 2006*, Ljubljana, Slovenia.

Thomas Rommel. 2008. Literary studies. In Ray Siemens and Susan Schreibman, editors, *A Companion to Digital Literary Studies*, Oxford. Blackwell.

Helmut Schmid. 1994. Probabilistic part-of-speech tagging using decision trees. In *International Conference on New Methods in Language Processing*, pages 44–49, Manchester, UK.

Michael Stubbs. 2005. Conrad in the computer: examples of quantitative stylistic methods. *Language and Literature*, 14(1):5–24.

Christopher Tribble. 2010. What are concordances and how are they used? In Anne O'Keeffe and Michael McCarthy, editors, *The Routledge Handbook of Corpus Linguistics*, pages 167–183, Abingdon. Routledge.

Dominic Widdows, Scott Cederberg, and Beate Dorow. 2002. Visualisation Techniques for Analysing Meaning. In *Fifth International Conference on Text, Speech and Dialogue (TSD-02)*, pages 107–114. Springer.

From high heels to weed attics: a syntactic investigation of chick lit and literature

Kim Jautze[*] **Corina Koolen**[†] **Andreas van Cranenburgh**[*†] **Hayco de Jong**[*]

[*]Huygens ING
Royal Dutch Academy of Science
P.O. box 90754, 2509 LT, The Hague, The Netherlands
{Kim.Jautze,Hayco.de.Jong}@huygens.knaw.nl

[†]Institute for Logic, Language and Computation
University of Amsterdam
Science Park 904, 1098 XH, The Netherlands
{C.W.Koolen,A.W.vanCranenburgh}@uva.nl

Abstract

Stylometric analysis of prose is typically limited to classification tasks such as authorship attribution. Since the models used are typically black boxes, they give little insight into the stylistic differences they detect. In this paper, we characterize two prose genres syntactically: chick lit (humorous novels on the challenges of being a modern-day urban female) and high literature. First, we develop a top-down computational method based on existing literary-linguistic theory. Using an off-the-shelf parser we obtain syntactic structures for a Dutch corpus of novels and measure the distribution of sentence types in chick-lit and literary novels. The results show that literature contains more complex (subordinating) sentences than chick lit. Secondly, a bottom-up analysis is made of specific morphological and syntactic features in both genres, based on the parser's output. This shows that the two genres can be distinguished along certain features. Our results indicate that detailed insight into stylistic differences can be obtained by combining computational linguistic analysis with literary theory.

1 Introduction

The gap between literary theory and computational practice is still great. Despite pleas for a more integrated approach (e.g., Ramsay, 2003), and suggestions from literary theorists (e.g., Roque, 2012), literary theory is more often used for illustrative or explicative purposes, rather than as a basis for computational analysis. The hermeneutic nature of most literary theory is a valid cause for caution, as it is not easy to 'translate' discursive arguments into the strict rules a computer needs. Too many intermediary steps are required, if a translation is possible at all.

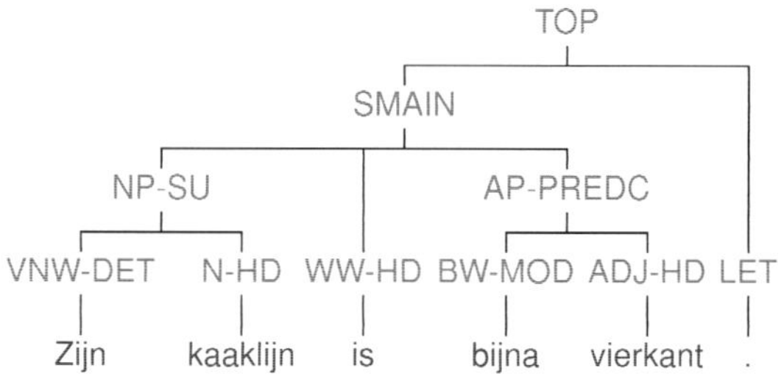

Figure 1: A sentence from 'Zoek Het Maar Uit' by Chantal van Gastel, as parsed by Alpino. Translation: *His jawline is almost square.*

We therefore take a different approach in this paper. Instead of building on hermeneutic theory, we use a literary-linguistic theory about syntactic structures as a basis for developing a computational method for prose genre analysis; in this paper we will focus on chick-lit and literary novels. Because of this tight connection between theory and method, these usually separate sections are combined. In addition to this top-down approach, we report bottom-up findings based on syntactic features encountered in the data. These complementary results will be used to further analyze and interpret genre differences, as opposed to author style. Our aim is not text categorization, but to describe the genres from a syntactic point of view.

We have chosen the genres of chick lit and literature, because many readers have intuitive notions on differences between them. In this paper we want to find out whether it is possible to retrace these notions in syntactic properties of the texts, by addressing the following questions: (i) are there differences in the distribution of sentence types between chick lit and literary novels, (ii) is the intuitive notion that chick lit is easier to read reflected in a tendency towards simple sentence structures rather than complex ones? In answering these questions, two methodological goals are achieved simultaneously: we discover how a specific literary-linguistic theory can be transformed to a computational method and we explore how well the output of a statistical parser facilitates such an investigation.

This study is a first exploration in a project called The Riddle of Literary Quality,[1] which aims to find patterns in the texts of Dutch current-day novels, that relate to the distinction between high-brow and low-brow literature. Deep syntactic structures as researched in the present paper are an important aspect of this investigation.

2 Theory and method

According to linguists Leech and Short (1981) syntactic structure is one of the grammatical features that can be taken into account when analyzing the style of prose texts. To this end, they make a division between six basic sentence types, from simple to parenthetic.

Toolan (2010) applies their theory by close-reading a paragraph from a short story by Alice Munro. He suggests that the six sentence types are part of a hierarchy of increasing complexity, a notion we will explore further by taking a distant reading approach, namely syntactically analyzing a prose corpus. In recent computational work on syntactic stylistics by Feng et al. (2012) and van Cranenburgh (2012) computational explorations of deep syntactic structures in academic and literary writing styles are undertaken on a similar scale. They make use of a machine learning methodology in which the results are evaluated on objective criteria, in this case authorship.

In line with this previous research we want to examine whether the use of certain types of sentence structures can inform our understanding of the difference between two prose genres, chick lit and literature. As opposed to Feng et al. (2012) however, we do not rely on black box machine learning approaches. And instead of extracting arbitrary syntactic patterns as in van Cranenburgh (2012), we target specific syntactic features, based partially on literary-linguistic theory as well as manual exploration of the data. To be more specific, the computational tools we employ deliver syntactic structures by querying the structures for certain syntactic features. During the development of our method, we continually verify our intuitions against the actual data.

To categorize the sentences into types, we devise two classifications, based on a combination of the theory developed by Leech and Short (1981) and Toolan (2010) and computational tests in Feng et al. (2012).

Class I

1. Simple: one main clause, no subordination on any level in the parse tree
2. Compound: coordination of sentence-level clauses, no subordination on any level
3. Complex: subordination anywhere in the sentence, no top-level coordination
4. Complex-compound: coordination on top-level and subordination

Leech and Short's definition does not specify whether non-finite or relative clauses that modify noun phrases count towards being a complex sentence. According to the ANS (2013), the Dutch standard reference work on grammar, all sentences with more than one connection between a subject and predicate are 'composed,' thus not 'singular' or simple. We therefore choose to count all subordinating clauses as making a sentence complex.

See (1)–(4) for examples of each sentence type.[2] An (L) indicates a sentence from the literature corpus, and a (C) a sentence from the chick lit corpus.

Simple sentence:

(1) a. Sjaak schraapte zijn keel. (L)
Sjaak cleared his throat.
b. Mijn knieën voelen als pudding. (C)
My knees feel like jelly.

Compound sentence:

(2) Ik had dood kunnen zijn en niemand deed iets. (C)
I could have died and no one did anything.

[1] Cf. http://literaryquality.huygens.knaw.nl

[2] These are examples from the novels in our corpus; cf. table 1.

Complex sentence:

(3) Ik weet ook niet waarom ik op van die hoge hakken ga shoppen. (C)
I really don't know why I go shopping on such high heels.

Complex-compound sentence:

(4) Suzan had een vaag gezoem gehoord terwijl ze bezig was in de keuken en had voor de zekerheid de deur opengedaan. (L)
Suzan had heard a vague buzzing while she was busy in the kitchen and had opened the door to be safe.

The second classification describes the distribution of several types of complex sentences, based on Toolan's hierarchical ordering of complex sentence types. This concerns sentences consisting of a dependent and main clause at the top level:

Class II

1. Trailing: main clause followed by subordinating clause
2. Anticipatory: subordinating clause followed by main clause
3. Parenthetic: subordinating clause interrupting a main clause

Toolan argues that the complex sentences, especially the anticipatory and parenthetic ones, are more demanding to process than the simple and compound sentences, because of a disruption in the linear clause-by-clause processing (Toolan, 2010, p. 321).

This can be explained by two principles: (1) the principle that theme precedes rheme (originally called 'Behaghel's second law') and (2) the 'complexity principle' (originally 'Law of increasing terms') (Behaghel, 1909). The first principle concerns the content: the less informative or important elements are placed before what is important or new. Usually, the new information is introduced by the subordinate clause and is therefore placed after the main clause. The second principle argues that generally the more complex and longer elements–'heavier' constituents containing more words and elaborate syntax–tend to be placed at the end of the sentence (Behaghel, 1909; Bever, 1970). These principles also apply to Dutch; cf. Haeseryn (1997, p. 308) and ANS (2013). With respect to the content and syntactic dependency, subordinate clauses are more demanding and complex, thus at best in this final position.

Trailing sentence

(5) Bo is te dik, omdat Floor hem macaroni voert.
Bo is too fat, because Floor feeds him macaroni.

Anticipatory sentence

(6) Omdat Floor Bo macaroni voert, is hij te dik.
Because Floor feeds Bo macaroni, he is too fat.

Parenthetic sentence

(7) Bo is, omdat Floor hem macaroni voert, te dik.
Bo, because Floor feeds him macaroni, is too fat.

We parse the corpus with the Alpino parser (Bouma et al., 2001; van Noord, 2006) to obtain syntactic parse trees (e.g., figure 1). The output of Alpino is in the form of dependency trees, containing both syntactic categories and grammatical functions. In order to work with tools based on constituency trees, we convert any non-local dependencies to discontinuous constituents, and apply the transformation described by Boyd (2007) to resolve discontinuities. For example, the Dutch equivalent of a phrasal verb such as "Wake [NP] up" might be parsed as a discontinuous `VP` constituent, but will be split up into two separate constituents `VP*0` and `VP*1`, bearing an implicit relation encoded in the label.

In order to categorize the parsed sentences in Class I and II, we build two different sets of queries: one for the trees wherein the main clause is a direct child of the TOP-node, and another for the parsed trees that introduce an extra node (DU) between the TOP and the main clause. The former are the 'regular' sentences that comprise approximately 67 % of the corpus, the latter are the so-called 'discourse units' (DUs) that comprise 33 %. DUs incorporate extensions to the sentence nucleus; cf. (8a) and (8b), constructions which depend on discourse relations (8c), and implicit conjunctions (8d).

(8) a. [$_{\text{DU}}$ [$_{\text{SMAIN-NUCL}}$ dat verbaast me] , [$_{\text{SAT}}$ dat je dat nog weet]]
that surprises me, that you still remember that

b. [$_{\text{DU}}$ [$_{\text{SMAIN-TAG}}$ Hij verklaarde] : [$_{\text{SMAIN-NUCL}}$ "Ik kom niet"]]
He declared: "I won't come"

c. [$_{\text{DU}}$ dus [$_{\text{SMAIN-NUCL}}$ Jan gaat naar huis.]]
So Jan is going home.

d. (welke kranten lees jij?) [$_{\text{DU}}$ [$_{\text{DU-DP}}$ bij de lunch de Volkskrant] ; [$_{\text{DU-DP}}$ s avonds de NRC]
(which newspapers do you read?) at lunch the Volkskrant; at night the NRC

(van Noord et al., 2011, p.182–192)

CHICK LIT	LITERATURE
Gastel, Chantal van - Zoek het maar uit (2011)	Beijnum, Kees van - De oesters van Nam Kee (2000)
Gastel, Chantal van - Zwaar verliefd (2009)	Beijnum, Kees Van - De Ordening (1998)
Harrewijn, Astrid - In zeven sloten (2007)	Dorrestein, Renate - Een sterke man (1994)
Harrewijn, Astrid - Luchtkussen (2009)	Dorrestein, Renate - Hart van steen (1998)
Hollander, Wilma - Bouzouki Boogie (2011)	Dorrestein, Renate - Het hemelse gerecht (1991)
Hollander, Wilma - Dans der liefde (2010)	Enquist, Anna - De Thuiskomst (2005)
Hollander, Wilma - Onder de Griekse zon (2008)	Enquist, Anna - De Verdovers (2011)
Middelbeek, Mariette - Revanche in New York (2006)	Enquist, Anna - Het meesterstuk (1994)
Middelbeek, Mariette - Single En Sexy (2009)	Glastra van Loon, Karel - De Passievrucht (1999)
Middelbeek, Mariette - Status O.K. (2010)	Glastra van Loon, Karel - Lisa's Adem (2001)
Verkerk, Anita - Als een zandkorrel in de wind (1994)	Grunberg, Arnon - De Asielzoeker (2003)
Verkerk, Anita - Bedrogen liefde (2006)	Grunberg, Arnon - Huid en haar (2010)
Verkerk, Anita - Cheesecake & Kilts (2010)	Japin, Arthur - De grote wereld (2006)
Verwoert, Rianne - Match (2009)	Japin, Arthur - Vaslav (2010)
Verwoert, Rianne - Schikken of stikken (2010)	Moor, Margriet de - De Schilder en het Meisje (2010)
Verwoert, Rianne - Trouw(en) (2009)	Moor, Margriet de - De verdronkene (2005)

Table 1: The corpus

The translation of Alpino-tags into queries is as follows (van Noord et al., 2011):

1. Categories for main clauses: SMAIN (declaratives), SV1 (verb initial: imperatives, polar questions) and WHQ (-questions).
2. Categories for finite subordinate clauses: SSUB (V-final), WHSUB (constituent questions), and (WH)REL (relative clauses).
3. Categories for non-finite subordinate clauses: PPART (perfect tense), INF (bare infinitives), TI (to-infinitives), and OTI ('om te' +) when accompanied by the BODY-function. Without BODY, PPART and INF can also be part of a simple sentence.
4. Functions used with DU: DP (discourse part), NUCL (sentence nucleus) SAT ("satellite" of the sentence, comparable with subordinate clauses)[3] and TAG (tag questions: 'isn't it?', 'you know?', dialogue markers: 'he said', etc.)

The query language used is TGrep2 (Rohde, 2005). For example, we identify simple sentences using the following query:

```
TOP !< DU < ( /SMAIN|SV1|WHQ/ !< /CONJ/ )
    !<< /WHSUB|SSUB|(PPART|TI|INF)-BODY/
```

This query matches a TOP node which does not have a DU child, but does have a SMAIN, SV1, or WHQ child. This child, in turn, must not have one of the categories signifying a conjunction or subordinate clause, at any level.

[3]The Alpino treebank annotation uses the terminology of nucleus and satellite, originally from Rhetorical Structure Theory (Mann and Thompson, 1988).

	chick lit	literature
no. of sentences	7064.31	7237.94
sent. length	11.90	**14.12**
token length	4.77	**4.98**
type-token ratio	0.085	**0.104**
time to parse (hrs)	2.05	**5.14**

Table 2: Basic statistics, mean by genre. Bold indicates a significant difference.

We test for statistical significance of the syntactic features with a two-tailed, unpaired t-test. We consider p-values under 0.05 to be significant. We present graphs produced by Matplotlib (Hunter, 2007), including standard deviations among texts of each genre.

3 Data

Our corpus is composed of 32 Dutch novels, equally divided between the genres chick lit and literature, and published between 1991 and 2011, cf. table 1. These novels were selected from a collection of ebooks; the number of each set was restricted by the number of chick-lit novels available. Female and male writers should ideally be equally represented, to avoid gender being a possible confounding factor. Since the chick-lit novels at our disposal were all written by women, this was not possible for that genre. The genre distinctions are based on classifications

	%	. %
simple	32.36	29.87
compound	8.54	6.23
complex	16.10	17.93
complex-compound	4.94	3.86
DU simple	5.98	4.56
DU compound	8.36	11.02
DU complex (compound or not)	7.64	**11.52**

Table 3: Sentence Class I identification, regular and DU-sentences. Bold indicates a significant difference.

by the publisher and reviews on `www.chicklit.nl`. For selecting literature we employed an additional criterion: the writer of the literary novel(s) has had to be accredited by winning at least one Dutch national literary prize.

Table 2 lists basic surface characteristics of the genres. A salient detail is that the literary novels took significantly longer to parse than the chick-lit novels ($p = 0.0001$), which cannot be attributed solely to longer sentence length, because the difference remains when correcting for the cubic time complexity of parsing—viz. $O(nm^3)$, with n the number of sentences, and m average sentence length.

4 Results on sentence types

Table 3 shows the results for Class I. The queries could classify approximately 60 % out of the 67 % regular sentences and 24.5 % out of the of 33 % discourse units into one of these four basic sentence types. Since DU-sentences often contain multiple main clauses without an explicit form of conjunction, it is difficult to define when a sentence is a compound rather than a complex sentence. Therefore we do not distinguish between compound and non-compound for complex DU-sentences, cf. 'DU complex' in table 3.

The remaining 15.5 % of the sentences in our corpus cannot be classified by our queries and would therefore fall into a residual category. This is (probably) due to single-word and verbless sentence fragments that do not fit into any of the categories and are therefore not captured by any of the formulated queries.

	%	. %
trailing	6.50	6.32
anticipatory	1.03	1.20
parenthetic	0.01	**0.03**

Table 4: Sentence Class II identification. Bold indicates a significant difference.

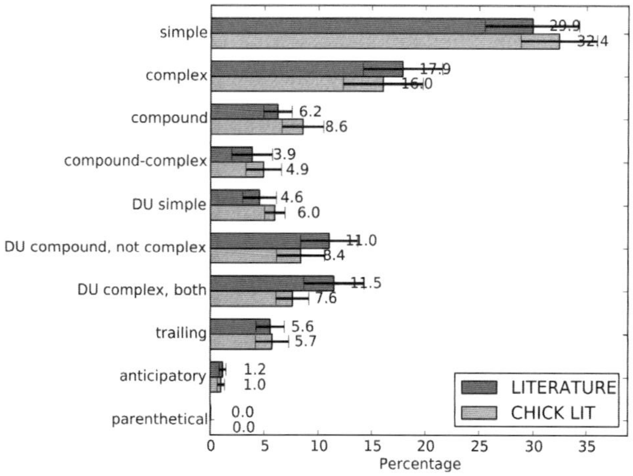

Figure 2: Overview of sentence tests.

The Class I identification shows that chick-lit authors tend to use more simple sentence structures and literary writers prefer complex ones, in both regular and DU-type sentences.[4] Although this difference is not significant for regular sentences, this may have been caused by the relatively small size of the corpus. In the discourse type-sentences DU complex (both with and without coordination) does show a significant difference. DU complex predicts genre adequately ($p = 0.003$; cf. figure 4), indicating that dialogue sentences might be a better predictor for genre differences than narrative sentences.

The results for Class II identification can be found in table 4. Although the difference is not significant, in chick lit we do find a tendency towards the use of more trailing sentences, as opposed to more anticipatory sentences in literary novels. The difference in use of parenthetic structure is significant

[4]When taking a closer look at the constituents, the TI, OTI and BODY-INF clauses are the exception, because they are more often used in chick-lit novels. TI and OTI introduce to-infinitives, e.g., I want *to sleep*, and the BODY-INFs are bare infinitive clauses. These three are the least complex of the subordinating clauses.

	chick lit %	. %
noun phrases	6.4	**8.0**
prepositional phrases	5.5	**6.5**
prep. phrases (modifiers)	2.2	**2.9**
relative clauses	0.32	**0.50**
diminutives (% of words)	0.79	0.49

Table 5: Tests on morphosyntactic features. Bold indicates a significant difference.

(p = 0.014), but because of the negligible number of occurrences, this is not a reliable predictor. Relating these results to Toolan's theory that sentence types of Leech and Short are ordered according to increasing complexity—i.e., that anticipatory and parenthetic sentences are more demanding to process and therefore more complex—this tendency could be an indicator of a measurably higher syntactic complexity in literary novels.

In sum, although not significantly different for regular sentences, the Class I and II identification show that the genres tend to differ in the distribution of sentence types and complexity. With more data, the other tests may show significant differences as well. Especially the complex discourse units are good predictors of the two genres. This is crucial as DUs in general appear to be characteristic of narrative text, which typically contain extensive dialogue and informal speech. However, not all dialogue is identified as a discourse unit, because we did no preprocessing to identify all sentences in quoted speech as being part of dialogue. Therefore, the actual amount of dialogue per novel remains unclear.

5 Results on morphosyntactic features

In addition to to the deep syntactic results based on the top-down approach, we take a closer look at the syntactic categories in the generated trees. The results can be found in figure 3 and table 5.

5.1 Relative clauses

Figure 5 shows a substantial difference in the number of relative clauses used in literature and chick lit (p=0.0005). Relative clauses modify noun phrases to describe or identify them. Therefore the relative clause makes the NP 'heavier'. The syntax prefers the relative clause to be placed directly after the NP,

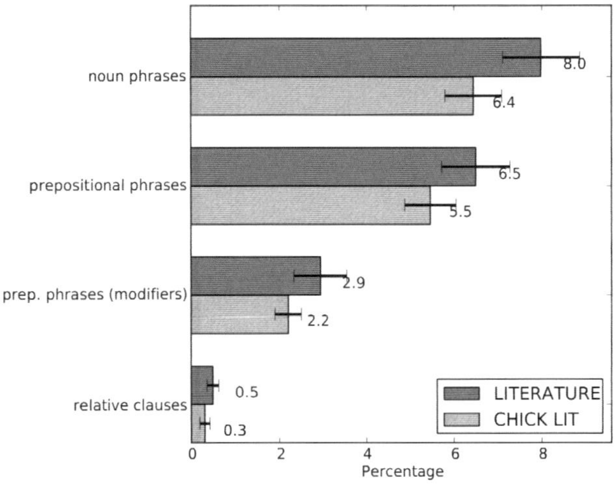

Figure 3: Overview of morphosyntactic tests.

although they may be extraposed for pragmatic reasons. When the NP is a subject, this causes the head noun of the NP to be distant from the main verb:

(9) De mensen [$_{REL}$ die even eerder nog zo rustig op de vloer hadden zitten mediteren], sprongen nu dansend en schreeuwend om elkaar heen. (L)
The people who just moments before had been meditating quietly on the floor, were now jumping around each other dancing and screaming.

The relative clause interrupts the relation between the subject and the predicate, but to a lesser extent than in a parenthetic sentence structure. With relative clauses there is also a disruption of the expected information flow, and this contributes to making such sentences more complex to process (Gibson, 1998).

Furthermore, the higher number of relative clauses in the literary novels makes the sentences more elaborate. In *Chick lit: the new woman's fiction* Wells argues a similar point to make a distinction between the genres:

> "[T]he language of chick-lit novels is unremarkable, in a literary sense. Richly descriptive or poetic passages, the very bread and butter of literary novels, both historical and contemporary, are virtually nonexistent in chick lit." (Wells, 2005, p. 65)

5.2 Prepositional phrases

Given the longer average sentence length of literature, it is to be expected that the prepositional phrases (PPs; as well as noun phrases; NPs) occur more frequently in literary novels than in chick lit (p = 0.0044 and

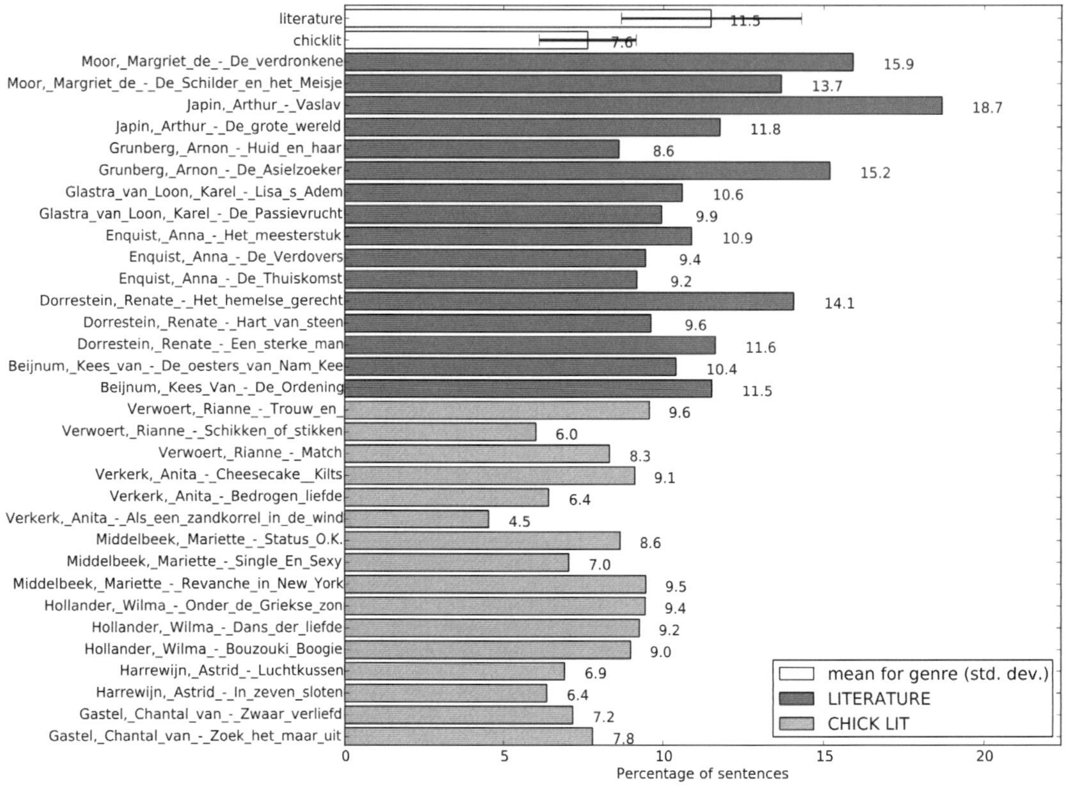

Figure 4: Distribution of complex DU-sentences.

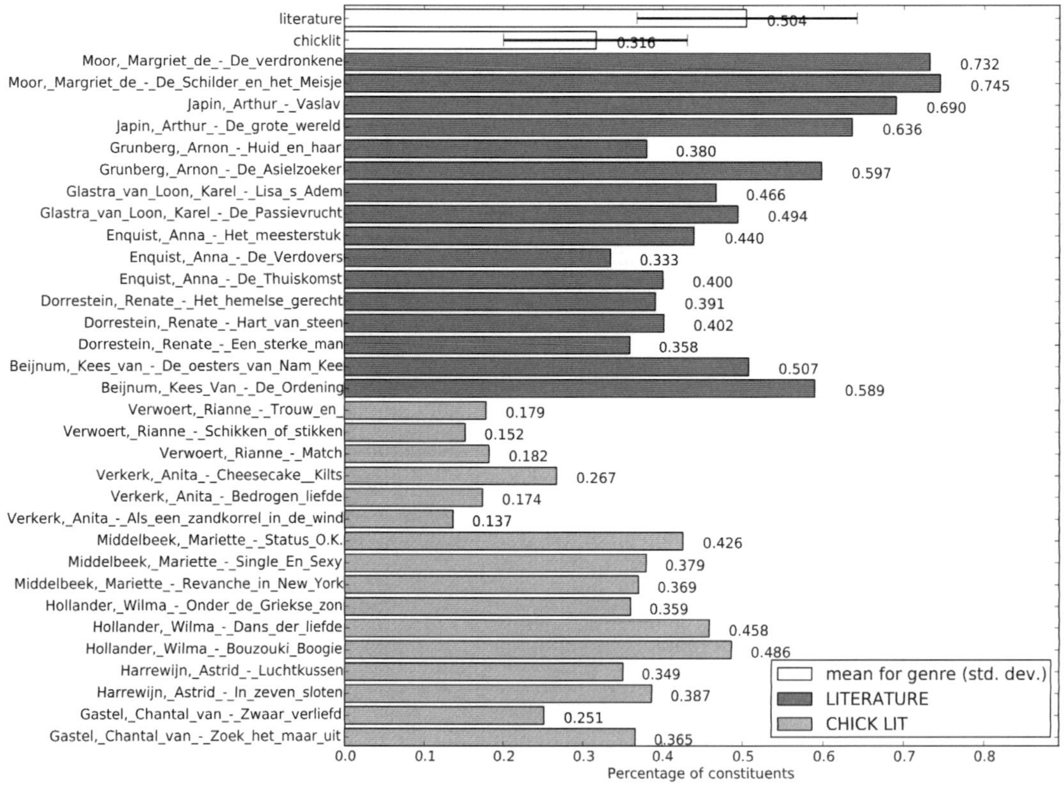

Figure 5: Relative clauses in each text.

p = 0.0015, respectively). The aforementioned argument by Wells that chick lit is less descriptive than literature is reflected in the results of the PPs and NPs as well. PPs, especially PP-adjuncts—grammatically optional constituents that function as modifiers of other constituents—are also indicative of descriptive language. Example (10) shows liberal use of prepositional phrases, including the first two PP-MODs that modify the same constituent—although the latter was not attached correctly by the parser.

(10) Ineens had ik zin om te schreeuwen en de gerookte zalm en quiches van tafel te slaan, [$_{\text{PP-MOD}}$ maar [$_{\text{MWU-HD}}$ in plaats daarvan]] troostte ik me [$_{\text{PP-PC}}$ met de wietzolder [$_{\text{PP-MOD}}$ van [$_{\text{N-OBJ1}}$ Emiel]], [$_{\text{PP-MOD}}$ met [$_{\text{NP-OBJ1}}$ de gedachte dat ik nog meer geheimen had en dat het behaaglijk kon zijn]] [$_{\text{NP-OBJ1}}$ het slappe geklets [$_{\text{PP-MOD}}$ van [$_{\text{N-OBJ1}}$ anderen]] te verachten] (L)
Suddenly I felt an urge to scream and throw the smoaked salmon and quiches off the table, but instead I consoled myself with the weed attic of Emiel, with the idea that I had yet more secrets and that it could be comfortable to despise the petty banter of others.

In sum, both the relative clauses and the PPs differentiate between literature and chick lit and point towards more descriptive language in literature.

5.3 Diminutives

Another marker for the distinction between chick lit and literature is the use of diminutives (almost significant, p=0.055). In Dutch, the diminutive is a productive part of the language and is typically formed by the suffix '-je'. Alpino marks such words with the morphological feature ' .' The frequent use of the diminutive is a common element in colloquial speech, and aside from the literal meaning of smallness diminutives are also used to express endearment, intimacy, and familiarity:

(11) Ik draai me om en pak mijn telefoontje. (C)
I turn around and take my telephone- .

This may indicate that language in chick lit is closer to real-life speech than that of literature and could be explored further when the speech-narrative distinction is operationalized.

6 Discussion

A starting point for further exploration is offered by our finding that the complex DU-sentences clearly differentiate between chick lit and literature. Something similar is suggested by Egbert (2012), who uses Multi-Dimensional analysis to explore literary styles. He identifies stylistic variation in the dimensions of Thought Presentation versus Description, and Dialogue versus Narrative. This finding supports our conclusion that it would be fruitful to pursue an intratextual distinction of regular versus dialogue sentences. In future research the method could for instance be expanded by using a discourse analyzer to identify all dialogue sentences. This will require some notion of a text grammar (Nunberg, 1990; Power et al., 2003), to recognize the different ways in which dialogue can be represented in text.

In order to assess the fitness of statistical parsers for literary investigations, a more comprehensive study of the quality of the parse trees is in order. The trees we have inspected were overall of good quality, especially concerning the elements we analyze. These consist mostly of overtly marked syntactic constituents, and do not hinge on correct attachments, which are often difficult to get right for statistical parsers.

Furthermore, we would like to investigate Toolan's claims about the complexity of sentence types, and on more specific morphosyntactic features. Unfortunately, little theory exists on syntactic aspects of literature, let alone its complexity. This could be improved by using results from psycholinguistics on what kinds of syntactic constructions are perceived as complex. Related to this is the work concerning readability measures, such as the Flesch and Kincaid scales, which can be obtained with the `style` program (Cherry and Vesterman, 1981).

Finally, in future work we would like to combine our computational results with literary interpretation. This requires attending to the context of the syntactic features in question.

7 Conclusion

We have operationalized a literary-linguistic theory by employing several computational tools and found specific syntactic features that characterize the two prose genres. Especially the Discourse Units showed a marked difference between the genres: chick lit uses more compound sentences, whereas literature contains more complex sentences. The bottom-up tests showed that chick-lit writers use significantly more diminutives, whereas literary writers employ more prepositional phrases and relative clauses which results in more descriptive language.

Although these findings agree with intuitive notions that literature employs more complex syntactic constructions than chick lit, computational analysis has proven its added value. The distant reading method of sifting through large amounts of text can reveal patterns too subtle or diffused to spot without computational tools; the distribution of the specific sentence structures we have investigated here would have been cumbersome to extract manually.

Our approach of analyzing syntactic features yields promising results on characterizing prose genre and explaining the syntactic differences. The positive results mean that the method that we have applied can be developed further in the context of the project The Riddle of Literary Quality to find out whether syntactic complexity correlates with the perceived aesthetic quality of the texts as well.

Acknowledgments

We are grateful to Isaac Sijaranamual for supplying us with a collection of ebooks and timely advice on pre-processing, and to Emy Koopman for suggestions on statistical matters. We thank Karina van Dalen-Oskam, Rens Bod, and Sally Wyatt for reading drafts, and the reviewers for helpful comments.

This paper is part of the project The Riddle of Literary Quality, supported by the Royal Netherlands Academy of Arts and Sciences as part of the Computational Humanities program.

References

ANS. 2013. Algemene Nederlandse Spraakkunst (ANS). URL http://ans.ruhosting.nl/.

Otto Behaghel. 1909. Beziehungen zwischen umfang und reihenfolge von satzgliedern. *Indogermanische Forschungen*, 25:110–142.

Thomas G. Bever. 1970. The cognitive basis for linguistic structures. In J.R. Hayes, editor, *Cognition and the Development of Language*, pages 279–362. Wiley, New York.

Gosse Bouma, Gertjan van Noord, and Robert Malouf. 2001. Alpino: Wide-coverage computational analysis of Dutch. *Language and Computers*, 37(1):45–59.

Adriane Boyd. 2007. Discontinuity revisited: An improved conversion to context-free representations. In *Proceedings of the Linguistic Annotation Workshop*, pages 41–44. URL http://aclweb.org/anthology/W/W07/W07-1506.

Lorinda L. Cherry and William Vesterman. 1981. Writing tools—the STYLE and DICTION programs. Computer Science Technical Report 91, Bell Laboratories, Murray Hill, N.J. Republished as part of the 4.4BSD User's Supplementary Documents by O'Reilly.

Jesse Egbert. 2012. Style in nineteenth century fiction: A multi-dimensional analysis. *Scientific Study of Literature*, 2(2):167–198.

Song Feng, Ritwik Banerjee, and Yejin Choi. 2012. Characterizing stylistic elements in syntactic structure. In *Proceedings of EMNLP*, pages 1522–1533. URL http://www.aclweb.org/anthology/D12-1139.

Edward Gibson. 1998. Linguistic complexity: locality of syntactic dependencies. *Cognition*, 68(1):1–76.

Walter Haeseryn. 1997. Achteropplaatsing van elementen in de zin. *Colloquium Neerlandicum*, 13:303–326.

John D. Hunter. 2007. Matplotlib: a 2D graphics environment. *Computing In Science & Engineering*, 9(3):90–95.

Geoffrey N. Leech and Michael H. Short. 1981. *Style in Fiction. A linguistic introduction to English fictional prose*. English Language Series 13. London / New York: Longman.

William C. Mann and Sandra A. Thompson. 1988. Rhetorical structure theory: Toward a functional theory of text organization. *Text*, 8(3):243–281.

Geoff Nunberg. 1990. *The Linguistics of Punctuation*. volume 18 in CSLI Lecture Notes. CSLI, Stanford, California.

Richard Power, Donia Scott, and Nadjet Bouayad-Agha. 2003. Document structure. *Computational Linguistics*, 29(2):211–260.

Stephen Ramsay. 2003. Toward an algorithmic criticism. *Literary and Linguistic Computing*, 18(2):167–174.

Douglas LT Rohde. 2005. *TGrep2 User Manual version 1.15*. Massachusetts Institute of Technology. URL http://tedlab.mit.edu/dr/Tgrep2.

Antonio Roque. 2012. Towards a computational approach to literary text analysis. In *Proceedings of the Workshop on Computational Linguistics for Literature*, pages 97–104. URL http://www.aclweb.org/anthology/W12-2514.

Michael Toolan. 2010. The intrinsic importance of sentence type and clause type to narrative effect: or, how Alice Munro's "Circle of Prayer" gets started. In *Language and style. In honour of Mick Short*, pages 311–327. Palgrave Macmillan, New York.

Andreas van Cranenburgh. 2012. Literary authorship attribution with phrase-structure fragments. In *Proceedings of the Workshop on Computational Linguistics for Literature*, pages 59–63. URL http://www.aclweb.org/anthology/W12-2508.

Gertjan van Noord. 2006. At last parsing is now operational. In *TALN06. Verbum Ex Machina. Actes de la 13e conference sur le traitement automatique des langues naturelles*, pages 20–42.

Gertjan van Noord, Ineke Schuurman, and Gosse Bouma. 2011. *Lassy Syntactic Annotation Manual*. URL http://www.let.rug.nl/vannoord/Lassy/sa-man_lassy.pdf.

Juliette Wells. 2005. Mothers of chick lit? Women writers, readers, and literary history. In Suzanne Ferriss and Mallory Young, editors, *Chick lit: the new woman's fiction*, pages 45–70. Routledge, New York.

Author Index